POORMAN'S NOSEGAY

Flowers from a Cottage Garden

by the same author

PEEPSHOW INTO PARADISE
A History of Children's Toys

LESLEY GORDON

Poorman's Nosegay

Flowers from a Cottage Garden

'For the Poorman's nosegay is an introduction
to a Prince.'

CHRISTOPHER SMART

COLLINS AND HARVILL PRESS
LONDON 1973

© 1973 Lesley Gordon
ISBN 0 00 262637 3
Set in Monotype Caslon

Made and Printed in Great Britain by
William Collins Sons & Co. Ltd, Glasgow
for Collins, St James's Place and
Harvill Press, 30A Pavillion Road,
London SW1

To S.R.E.

Contents

Colour Plates

Plates in Black and White

PART I

Poorman's Nosegay

'These sweet herbs and flowers for nosegays shall be set in order upon beds and quarters of such-like length and breadth as those of the kitchen garden.'

GERVASE MARKHAM

'Reader,

May the Bookseller have so much Profit in the selling it, and thou the same Pleasure and Profit in buying it, that has accrued to me by Collecting and Experience therein; I am thine to serve.'

LEONARD MEAGER, 1699

Poorman's Nosegay

Our Poorman's Nosegay contains flowers of all seasons –
tulips with marigolds, snowdrops with roses – but for this we
have precedent in the unsurpassable flower paintings of the
seventeenth and eighteenth centuries. They have a right to be
included for these reasons: they are pickable, they are common,
they are vigorous, and they have been loved for as long as
cottage gardens have existed. Taken from the woods and
fields and hedgerows, brought from distant lands by mission-
aries and crusaders, they have rooted in town and country
gardens. They have flourished because of the love and care
bestowed on them, and they have flourished in spite of neglect.
From them finer and rarer flowers have been raised which
have no place here. Here you will find no rarities and no tender
flowers, only the sturdy yeomen stock of the cottage plot.

Neither is it a posy of wild flowers, although somewhere,
and at some time, they all sprang from the wild, and many do
so still. Some, like the primrose and the violet, seem as happy in
the woods or meadow as they do in a garden, but most respond
to care and attention, and show their gratitude by longer
stems or larger and more deeply coloured, or sometimes
doubled, flowers. If a date can be given for this change, it lies
somewhere between the publication of Gerard's *Herball* in
1597, where most of the flowers illustrated are small, self-
coloured and single, and the appearance of John Parkinson's
Paradisi in Sole Paradisus Terrestris in 1629, where cultivation
is already made evident in the engravings of striped and
doubled flowers.

Many of the Poorman's flowers are scented, for a true
nosegay, as its name implies, was for holding to the nose.
Sweet-smelling flowers and herbs were needed, not so much
for their appeal to the eye, as to mask the unpleasant odours of
the streets and houses. Rosemary and lavender, for instance,

were used as 'strewing' herbs, and Parkinson says of germander and hyssop that 'they must be kept in some form and proportion with cutting, and the cuttings are much used as a strawing herb for houses, being pretty and sweet.'

Roses, marigolds, myrtle, stock and mignonette as well were 'cried' by the street sellers, many of whom had grown the flowers in their own small gardens.

> Come buy my fine roses,
> My myrtles and stocks,
> My sweet-smelling blossoms
> And close-growing box,
>
> Here's my fine rosemary, sage and thyme,
> Come buy my ground ivy,
> Here feverfew, gilliflowers and rue
> Come buy my knotted marjoram, ho!
>
> Come buy my mint, my fine green mint,
> Here's fine lavender for your cloathes,
> Here's parseley and winter savoury
> And heart's-ease which all do choose.[1]

These and many other cries could be heard through the summer days from dawn till dusk, and indeed, lavender was still 'cried' within living memory.

Sometimes these humble vendors of flowers or fruit rose to higher and more worldly things, leaving their wares to other mongers to cry, as Nell left her oranges. Such a one was Fanny Barton, Nosegay Fan of Vinegar Yard, who scratched a living selling flowers in the Mall. This bright-eyed, motherless child left her father's cobbler's shop each evening, whether with parental consent we are not told, making her way to the Bedford and the Piazza coffee-houses to entertain the young bloods who frequented these places.

Later, to better herself, she became a milliner in Cockspur Street, and from there graduated to the stage, where she played at the Haymarket and Drury Lane. In 1759 she married and returned to the stage as the famous Mrs Abington, but her marriage was short-lived. She was the friend of Doctor Johnson and of Horace Walpole, yet when her looks and her money dwindled she found herself alone. She died in 1815, and was buried in the churchyard of St James's, Piccadilly. No one attended her funeral, and not a flower was dropped on the grave of Nosegay Fan.

At much the same time, another little Nosegay Fan, Fanny Murray, was earning her living by selling flowers in the streets of Bath. She would stand with her basket in the Abbey Yard to catch the fine ladies on their way to their early morning bathe, for it was the fashion then to enter the water carrying a nosegay. Fanny Murray, like Fanny Barton, sold more than flowers, but she died a faithful wife at last, at the age of forty-nine.

Richard Weston, in 1773, wrote advising flower growers that 'The flowers for nosegays are quite the common sorts, which require little culture; they should in general be such as are sweet scented.'[2]

Not only were sweet-smelling herbs strewn on the floors of cottage and castle, but in the larger dwellings they were placed about the rooms in bough-pots, or beau-pots, and made up into bunches for wearing. These beau-pots were probably of Norman French origin, and less than a hundred years ago the term was still in use in country districts.

Deborah, the daughter of John Milton, wrote in her diary of the anxious and hurried time when the family left for Chalfont to avoid the plague, leaving their old Nurse Jellycot in charge of their house in Bunhill Fields. 'She (Nurse Jellycot) has tidied up the little Chamber over the House-door she means to occupy, and sett on the Mantell a Beau-pot of fresh Flowers she brought with her. The whole house smells of aromatick Herbs, we have burnt soe many of late for fumigation.'[3]

On 10 July, 1748, Lady Mary Wortley-Montague wrote from Italy to her daughter, Lady Bute, 'I have fitted up this farm house a room for my selfe, that is to say, strewed the floor with Rushes, cover'd the chimney with moss and branches,

21

and adorn'd the Room with Basons of earthen ware (which is made here to great perfection) fill'd with Flowers, and put in some straw chairs and a Couch Bed, which is my whole Furniture.'

Flowers growing in pots, both inside and outside the house, can be seen in old manuscripts. Fresh herbs were put down when company was expected, and growing plants in pots were brought in. Potted plants also played an important part in gardens already full of growing things. Window boxes were used too. Sir Hugh Platt[4] advises rosemary, sweet briar, bay and germander for the more shady parts of the room.

A Dutchman travelling in England in the sixteenth century wrote, 'Their chambers and parlours strewed over with sweet herbes refreshed mee; their nosegays finely intermingled with sundry sorts of fragrant flowers in their bedchambers and privy rooms with comfortable smell cheered me up and entirely delighted all my senses.'[5]

Women derived pleasure as they do now, from gathering and arranging flowers.

> This maiden in a morn betime,
> Went forth when May was in her prime,
>   to get sweet Cetywall*
> The honeysuckle, the Harlock,
> The Lily and the Lady-smock,
>   to deck her summer hall.[6]

Flowering grasses were sometimes used for beautifying the bedposts in time of sickness.

> So did the maidens with their various flowers
> Deck up their windows, and make neat their bowers,
> Used such cunning, as they did dispose
> The ruddy piny with the lighter rose,
> The monkshood with the bugloss, and entwine
> The white, the blue, the flesh-like columbine
> With pinks, sweet-williams; that far off the eye
> Could not the manner of their mixture spy.[7]

* Valerian.

In some parts of Europe, peasants never entered a church without an offering of flowers in season, a *bouquet d'église*, and small posies were left at wayside shrines; snowdrops for Our Lady at Candlemas; lilies for the Visitation; love-in-a-mist for St Catherine; camomile for St Anne, and the Christmas rose for St Agnes. Legends grew round these flowers, and were carried from place to place by pilgrims. People kept a corner of their cottage gardens especially for the growing of church posies and nosegays, and one old Essex woman was heard to refer to 'ordinary gays', the wild flowers, and 'garden gays', those which grew in her own small plot.

Guests were presented with posies on arrival and on departure, a pleasant custom. Flowers such as violets, primroses and marigolds were often used to decorate as well as to flavour food. Under the heading of 'Provisions and Products of June,' in Quintinye's *The Complete Gard'ner*, there is, 'Abundance of Flowers, as well to garnish Dishes, as to set out flower Pots, viz: Double Poppies of all colours, white, pale, violet, flesh-colour'd or Carnation, flame coloured, purple, violet colour'd, and panached or striped yellow, and violet Pansies, Lark's Heels, Fraxilenes or Fraxinellas, or Bastard Dittanies, Roses, of all sorts . . . and you begin to see some Cabbages.'

From Cabbages to Kings, or at least to a Chevalier and a Countess, and a rich man's nosegay.

CHEVALIER: I have always been fond of Flowers, but my Idea of their Merit was too mean and imperfect; I considered them as little productions that were accidentally scattered over the Earth. But I am now sensible they make their Appearance to please me, and I regard them with Admiration and Gratitude . . .

COUNTESS: The Festivals in the Country are never celebrated without Garlands, and the Entertainments of the Polite are usher'd in by a Flower. If the Winter denies them that Gratification, they have to recourse to Art. A young Bride, in all the Magnificence of her nuptial Array, would imagine she wanted a necessary part of her Ornaments, if she did not improve them with a Sprig of Flowers. A Queen amidst the greatest Solemnities, tho' she is cover'd with the Jewels of the Crown, has an Inclination to this rural Ornament; she is not satisfied with mere Grandeur and Majesty, but is desirous of assuming an Air of Softness and Gaiety, by the Mediation of Flowers.[8]

Mayday celebrations were especially a time for flowers.

> Always be merry if thou may,
> But waste not thy good alway:
> Have hat of flowers fresh as May,
> Chapelet of roses on Whitsunday.
> For sich array ne costneth but lyte,[9]

The Mayday nosegay became a 'garland' and assumed giant proportions, carried at the head of a procession of singing, dancing youth. Smaller groups of children carrying less imposing 'garlands' on sticks would break off from the main procession, calling from house to house, and doing a bit of business on the side. William Allingham mentioned them in his diary of 1882: 'Witley. May Day. – Overcast. A few cottage children came in carrying sticks with flowers tied to them – neither sung nor spoke, but stood shyly holding their flower sticks; got 6d. and went away. A curiously silent folk, the English peasants.'

Another floral custom, the pin-a-sight, could be viewed at bargain price, for the charge was only a pin. I remember these flower peepshows from my own childhood, and the formidable rows of pins that we stuck in our gym-slips as a proof of our artistic and commercial success. Flora Thompson describes these in *Larkrise to Candleford*:

Sometimes in the summer the 'pin-a-sight' was all the rage, and no girl would feel herself properly equipped unless she had one secreted about her. To make a 'pin-a-sight' two small sheets of glass, a piece of brown paper, and plenty of flowers were required. Then the petals were stripped from the flowers and arranged on one of the sheets of glass with the other sheet placed over it to form a kind of floral sandwich, and the whole was enveloped in brown paper, in which a little square window was cut, with a flap left hanging to act as a drop scene. Within the opening there appeared a multi-coloured medley of flower petals, and that was a 'pin-a-sight'. No design was aimed at; the object being to show as many and as brightly coloured petals as possible; but Laura when alone, loved to arrange her petals as little pictures, building up a geranium or a rose, or even a little house, against a background of green leaves.

Usually the girls only showed their 'pin-a-sights' to each other; but sometimes they would approach one of the women, or knock at a door, singing:

A pin to see a pin-a-sight;
All the ladies dressed in white.
A pin behind and a pin before,
And a pin to knock at a lady's door.

Bridal bouquets for rich and poor had never been the elaborate creations that are expected today. Small bunches of flowers passed between couples at their betrothal, and were worn as a sign of their engagement, and a simple posy was carried by the bride at her wedding. House and church were decorated as well, but until the Victorians introduced their tightly packed posies composed of circles of flowers without leaves, slightly raised in the centre, and bordered with paper lace, flower arrangements had always been of the simplest, even in the great houses. Here are the flowers ordered by the fourth Earl of Dorset for the wedding of his son at Knole. At the top of the bill of fare for the wedding it reads: 'To have fresh bowls in every corner and flowers tied upon them, and sweet briar, stock, gilly-flowers, pinks, wallflowers and any other sweet flowers in glasses and pots in every window and chimney.'[10]

But it is the Poorman's Nosegay which concerns us, and great was the pride with which he and his family wore their home-grown buttonholes on festive occasions. He knew every flower with its simple country name, as he knew the names of his own children. Had he not planted them, and watered them, and grown the choicest specimens to be worn at weddings and christenings, or on the squire's birthday? Even the highwayman carried his nosegay as he bumped his way over the cobbles in his execution cart to his hanging at Tyburn, for it was the usual practice for a malefactor to be sent on his last journey with a large bouquet, handed from the steps of St Sepulchre by some sobbing prostitute. Opera lovers will remember Polly Peachum's anguished cry when she pictures the fate of her beloved villain, Macheath, 'Methinks I see him already in the Cart, sweeter and more lovely than the Nosegay in his Hand.'[11] Stephens, in *A plaine Country Bridegroom*, reverses the coin with his picture of a reluctant lover, 'He shews neere affinity betwixt Marriage and Hanging: and to that purpose he provides a great Nosegay, and shakes hands with every one he meets, as if he were now preparing for a condemned Man's Voyage.'

Yet there came a time when the wearing of flowers was out of fashion, for Henry Phillips, the flower historian, wrote in 1824, 'Fashion does not at present sanction any but coachmen in wearing nosegays in this country, yet it has not influence sufficient to banish flowers from the garden, since we notice that those who have only a small piece of land attached to their dwellings, generally devote it to the service of Flora.'[12]

Fashion, as we know, is fickle, and the flower returned to favour. In 1848, an article by Thomas Miller for *The Illustrated London News* describes the flower sellers of Covent Garden market:

These itinerent dealers who make the streets of London ring with the pleasant spring-cry of 'All a-blowing, all a-growing!' as they move along with barrow, basket, and cart, are generally supplied from this market; and few would credit the many hundreds of pounds expended in the metropolis for the purchase of flower-roots to be replanted in the little back-yards called gardens, which are a peculiar feature in most of the London streets, beyond the city boundaries. Places which, to pass in front, a stranger would think no green thing had ever grown for years near such a neighbourhood; yet in the rear they contain choice wallflowers, sweet-williams, carnations, Canterbury-bells, hollyhocks, sun-flowers, and fancy dahlias, which have been grown within a mile or so of the bridges, and have been sent forth to 'dispute the prize' at a flower show.

. . . Our Covent Garden portresses – sturdy daughters of Erin, clad in almost manly attire, and with scarcely an exception, every soul a smoker and drinker of neat gin . . . Their faithfulness and honesty are deserving of the highest praise: no matter how valuable the load may be that you purchase, or how great the distance it has to be borne into the suburbs, you have but to pay the trifle agreed upon, furnish the right address, and when you return home, there you will find every bud and blossom un-injured, for Biddy may be trusted with uncounted gold. They are all a sturdy, short-necked race, moving caryatides, strong enough to support a temple . . . It requires a strong-armed man to help to replace the load upon their heads when they have rested; and few gentlemen, we hope, resist the appeal of 'Will your honour plase to lend a lift to the basket?'

Henry Mayhew, also, described the life of a flower-seller in 1851. 'At about seven years of age the girls first go into the streets to sell. A shallow-basket is given to them, with about two shillings for stock-money, and they hawk, according to the time of year, either oranges, apples, or violets; some begin their street education with the sale of water-cresses.' And the early morning scene in Covent Garden: 'Flower-girls, with large bundles of violets under their arms, run past, leaving a trail of perfume behind them . . . The pump in the market is now surrounded by a cluster of clattering wenches quarrelling over whose turn it is to water their drooping violets, and on the steps of Covent Garden Theatre are seated the shoeless girls, tying up the halfpenny and penny bundles.'[13]

Here, in contrast, is a comfortable picture of the sunny side of the Edwardian street: 'the bright harness of horses jangling as they champ the bit, a knot of flowers at every bridle; flower-sellers with baskets at all convenient corners, and along a road-way carts of palms and growing plants bending and waving in the wind; every man one meets has got his button-hole, and every maiden wears her posy; even the butcher-boy holds a bud between his thumb and finger, twirling it and smelling at it as he goes.'[14]

And in the country, too, women in tightly-buttoned hunting jackets, wearing equally tightly packed posies of violets, for violets were an important part, almost a symbol, of the Edwardian scene; pinned on to guipure lace; tucked into waistbelts; nestling in furs – 'Vi -lets, penny a bunch!', offering a precarious living to the Eliza Doolittles of London.

The Cottage Plot

'The Rich admire flowers; the Poor adore them.'

NEWMAN FLOWER

The Cottage Plot

From garden gays to the gay gardens where they grew; not the rich man's garden, for many sumptuous coffee-table books have been written on its history, nor even 'well-to-do' gardens, but the cottage garden, where men and women grew simple flowers that scarcely changed through the generations; for the history and pictures of this mini-paradise seldom find their way into books.

In the ancient world gardening was considered the work of slaves, and slaves had no gardens of their own. Many lives were spent in planting, weeding, watering, pleaching, and the elaborate topiary work of rich men's gardens, before humble folk acquired small plots for their own and their families' enjoyment. The Romans brought some knowledge of gardening with them when they built their villas in this country, but when the legions left, the gardens disappeared.

In the monasteries, monks tended their orchards and grew herbs and vegetables, carrying back from the surrounding countryside wild flowers to cultivate for their healing properties and perfumes, and for decorating the churches at festivals. Travellers would bring home strange plants from their pilgrimages abroad; seeds and cuttings were exchanged, and gradually flowers began to be valued for their beauty as well as for their usefulness. 'So curious and cunning are our Gardeners now in these daies, that they presume to doo in manner what they list with nature, and moderate hir course in things as if they were hir superiours.'[1]

It was after the Wars of the Roses, when England at last enjoyed such peace and prosperity as she had never before known, that the art of gardening really began.

> The helmet now an hive for bees becomes,
> And hilts of swords may serve for spiders' looms,

> Sharp pikes may make
> Teeth for a rake;
> And the keen blade, th'arch enemy of life,
> Shall be degraded to a pruning knife.
> The rustic spade
> Which first was made
> For honest agriculture, shall retake
> Its primitive employment, and forsake
> The rampires steep
> And trenches deep.
> Tame conies in our brazen guns shall breed,
> Or gentle doves their young ones there shall feed.
> In musket barrels
> Mice shall raise quarrels
> For their quarters. The ventriloquious drum,
> Like lawyers in vacations, shall be dumb.
> Now all recruits
> But those of fruits,
> Shall be forgot; and th' unarmed soldier
> Shall only boast of what he did whilere,
> In chimney's ends
> Among his friends.[2]

In time the old garden containing flowers grown for medicinal purposes only vanished, and gardening for pleasure crept in almost unnoticed. Herbs for 'sallets' grew among the fruit bushes, and flowers where they could; up to the cottage doors, and climbing by way of the porch to bedroom windows. Even the roof itself at times gave hospitality to wallflower, snapdragon and wild pink, until cottage and **garden were one**.

> I have a garden plot,
> Wherein there wants nor herbs, nor roots, nor flowers,
> Flowers to smell, roots to eat, herbs for the pot,
> And dainty shelters when the welkin lours:
> Sweet smelling beds of lilies and of roses,
> Which rosemary banks and lavender encloses.[3]

Inside, window-sills had their pot plants, and outside there were window boxes and baskets, until sometimes it almost seemed as though the cottage itself had sprung from the soil. Mary Russell Mitford described such a garden in *Our Village*. 'The pride of my heart and the delight of my eyes is my garden. Our House, which is in dimensions very much like a bird-cage, and might with almost equal convenience be laid on a shelf or hung up in a tree, would be utterly unbearable in warm weather, were it not that we have a retreat out of doors – and a very pleasant retreat it is.'

Such neatness above ground; such a tangle of roots beneath – roots that pushed and grasped and sucked the soil while men were born and died above them and the centuries went by.

> And where the Majoram once, and Sage and Rue,
> And Balm and Mint, with curl'd-leaf Parsley grew,
> And double Marigolds, and silver Thyme,
> And Pumpkins 'neath the window climb;
> And where I often, when a child, for hours
> Tried through the pales to get the tempting flowers,
> As Lady's-laces, Everlasting Peas,
> True-love-lies-bleeding, with the Hearts-at-ease,
> And Golden-rods, And Tansy running high,
> That o'er the pale tops smiled on passers-by,
> Flowers in my time which every one would praise,
> Though thrown like weeds from gardens nowadays. [4]

Eighteenth-century travellers were as admiring of English cottage gardens as twentieth-century tourists are today. Washington Irving wrote in his *Sketch Book*: 'The very labourer, with his thatched cottage and narrow slip of ground, attends to their embellishment. The trim hedge, the grass-plot before the door, the little flower-bed bordered with snug box, the woodbine trained up against the wall, and hanging its blossoms about the lattice, the pot of flowers in the window, the holly, providentially planted about the house, to cheat winter of its dreariness, and to throw in a semblance of green summer to cheer the fireside: all these bespeak the influence of taste.'

William Cobbett compared the gardens of Suffolk with those of the southern counties. 'It is curious, too, that though the people, I mean the poorer classes of people, are extremely neat in their houses, and though I found all their gardens dug up and prepared for cropping, you do not see about their cottages, (and it is just the same in Norfolk) that ornamental gardening; the walks and the flower borders, and the honey-suckles and roses trained over the doors or over arched sticks, that you see in Hampshire, Sussex, and Kent, that I have many a time sitten upon my horse to look at so long and so often, as greatly to retard me on my journey.'[5]

It may be that the gardeners were stung into activity by Cobbett's criticism. At all events, today there are pink roses spilling over the flint walls of Norfolk, and in the spring generous borders of daffodils, wallflowers and aubrieta outside the garden territories and bordering the roads of Suffolk and Essex, apparently unmolested by vandals; a form of generosity which would have warmed old Cobbett's heart, as it does mine.

The gardens surrounding halls and manor houses changed with fashion and the introduction of new plants, but cottages, within and without, remained unaffected by passing whim. Perhaps the only eighteenth- and early nineteenth-century plants that cottagers took to their hearts and their gardens were the fuchsia, the geranium, the flowering currant and the musk. Cobbett noted on one of his English tours that 'in Kent, Sussex, Surrey and Hampshire, and indeed in almost every part of England, that most interesting of all objects, that which is such an honour to England, and that which distinguishes it from all the rest of the world, namely, *those neatly kept and productive little gardens round the labourers' houses*, which are seldom unornamented with more or less of flowers.'[5]

Thomas Bewick's incomparable engravings of rural life show us many a small cottage, deep-set in trees, seeming almost to grow by the side of some deeply-rutted lane, or at a common's edge. Towards the end of his life he wrote of them in his memoirs: 'Here and there on this common were to be seen the cottage, or rather hovel, of some labouring man, built at his own expense, and mostly with his own hands; and to this he always added a garth and a garden, upon which great pains and labour were bestowed to make both productive; and for this purpose not a bit of manure was suffered to be wasted away on the "lonnings" or public roads.'[6]

New practical gardening knowledge came with the Huguenot refugees from the Low Countries, when they settled around London and Norwich. England owes much to these skilled and industrious workers, who more than repaid our hospitality by the knowledge of plant breeding that they brought with them. It was they who started the first gardening societies in this country.

With the advance in education, books were written directed particularly to the owners of cottage gardens. Here is some solemn advice, which I hope did not prove too daunting, to the young gardener. It is more than likely that his father would have been unable to read these well-meant exhortations, however strong the terms.

Advice to the Young Gard'ner,
On Planting and Rural Ornament.

But before the young planter puts his foot upon the spade, we beg leave to caution him, in the strongest terms, against *a want of spirit* in Planting. A slovenly Planter ranks among the most extravagant order of slovens: the labour, the plants, and the ground are thrown away, besides the consequent disgrace, not only to the individual, but to the Art itself.[7]

Nor did these self-imposed guides hesitate to grade their readers' gardens into 'degrees' of humbleness. 'I have written thus far in the hope of helping the humblest class of cottagers in the management of their flower borders; but, as I have previously remarked, there are degrees in cottage gardens and gardeners.'[8]

Could patronage go much further? But not all gardeners were humble. 'The great men's gardeners, great men themselves, kept flowers in the plot of ground about their cottages; gave out a seed or so here and there; talked garden gossip at the village ale-house'[9] and help and advice, and a cutting or two were given by the parson, or his wife, to their worthy parishioners, and the spread of good cottage gardening was insured.

When the landscape gardener took over the rich man's garden, flowering plants were banished to the kitchen plot, and many flower refugees barely escaped with their lives. Some may have disappeared forever — 'Others have taken refuge by the stable and the coach-house, near the low door of the kitchen or the cellar, where they crowd humbly like importunate beggars hiding their bright dresses among the weeds and holding their frightened perfumes as best they may, so as not to attract attention. . . . They fled to the farms, the cemetries, the little gardens of the rectories, the old maids' houses and country convents . . . seeking oblivion of the oldest villages.'[10]

In that most romantic of all places, a deserted garden, if you search among the docks and plantains, sometimes it may be possible to find, tangled among the couch-grass and half-hidden by nettles, a forgotten flower, common once, but today a rarity. A. C. Benson once had that delight, although in his case it was not some wan little half-hidden lingerer, but a garden flower escaped from captivity and run riot in congenial freedom outside its wonted bounds.

I have made friends with a new flower. If it had a simple and wholesome English name, I would like to know it, though I do not care to know what ugly and clumsy title the botany books may give it; but it lives in my mind, a perfect and complete memory of brightness and beauty, and, as I have said, a friend.

We had travelled far that day and were comfortably weary; we found a sloping ledge of turf upon which we sat, and presently became aware that on the little space of grass between us and the cliff must once have stood a cottage and a cottage garden. There was a broken wall behind us, and the little platform still held some garden flowers sprawling wildly, a stunted fruit bush or two, a knotted apple tree.

My own flower, or the bushes on which it grew, had once, I think, formed part of the cottage hedge; but it had found a wider place to its liking, for it ran riot everywhere; it scaled the cliff, where, too, the golden wall-flowers of the garden had gained a footing; it fringed the sand-patches beyond us, it rooted itself firmly in the shingle. On many of the bushes it was not yet fully out, and showed only in an abundance of small lilac balls, carefully folded; but just below me a cluster had found the sun and the air too sweet to resist, and had opened to the light. The flower was of a delicate veined purple, a five pointed star, with a soft golden heart. All the open blossoms stared at me with a tranquil gaze, knowing I would not hurt them.[11]

Botanists may instantly recognize this description and give a name, a wholesome English name, I hope, to this purple star, but I am content to accept and remember it, as Benson's Friend.

And the ancestors of those familiar 'ordinary' flowers, that still crowd old cottage gardens today? Looking back over the years we can see that

They were very few, no doubt, and very small and very humble, scarce to be distinguished from those of the roads, the fields and the glades. Have you ever observed the poverty and the monotony most skilfully disguised, of the floral decoration of the finest miniatures in our old manuscripts? Again, the pictures in our museums, down to the end of the Renascence period, have only five or six types of flowers, incessantly repeated, wherewith to enliven the richest palaces, the most marvellous views of Paradise. Before the sixteenth century, our gardens were almost bare; and, later, Versailles itself, Versailles the splendid, could have shown us only what the poorest village shows today. Violet, Daisy, Lily of the Valley, Marigold, Poppy, Crocus, Iris, Foxglove, Valerian, Larkspur, Forgetmenot, Wallflower, Rose still almost a Sweetbriar, and Lily.[10]

Maeterlinck, of course, was indulging in a little floral romancing when he describes the poverty and monotony so

37

skilfully disguised. Why should disguise be necessary, however skilful? With no foresight of the glories to come, the early painters must have delighted in their prim daisies, delicate heartsease and neat pinks; and delighted too in their increasing powers of depicting so faithfully, in colours patiently ground by hand, these simple flowers, still so fresh that it seems after centuries that you could pick them from the page as from a meadow. Their satisfaction in their skill and its dedication to God, must have been as deep a joy to them as the flowers themselves.

And so, leaf by leaf and flower by flower, the cottage gardens grew.

[The cottages] stand among, and are wrapped in, flowers as in a garment — rose and vine and creeper and clematis. They are mostly thatched, but some have tiled roofs, their deep, dark red clouded and stained with lichen and moss; and these roofs, too, have their flowers in summer. They are grown over with yellow stonecrop, that bright cheerful flower that smiles down at you from the lowly roof above the door, with such an inviting expression, so delighted to see you no matter how poor and worthless a person you may be or what mischief you may have been at, that you begin to understand the significance of a strange vernacular name of this plant — Welcome-home-husband-though-never-so-drunk.

But its garden flowers, clustering and nestling round it, amid which its feet are set — they are to me the best of all flowers. These are the flowers we know and remember forever. The old, homely, cottage-garden blooms, so old that they have entered the soul . . . fragrant gilly-flower and pink and clove-smelling carnation; wallflower, abundant periwinkle, sweet-william, larkspur, love-in-a-mist, and love-lies-bleeding, old woman's nightcap, and kiss-me-John-at-the-garden-gate, sometimes called pansy.[12]

A century passed, not so long in the life of a cottage garden — only a hundred blossomings — and A. E. Coppard knew the familiar satisfaction: 'The scent of wallflowers and lilac came to him as sweet almost as a wedge of newly-cut cake. The may bloom on his hedge drooped over the branches like crudded cream, and the dew in the gritty road smelled of harsh dust in a way that was pleasant. Well, if the cottage wasn't much good, the bit of a garden was all right.'[13]

> In Spring or in Autumn or any brave season,
> The flowers and bushes lose all sense of reason.
> They grow, if you please, with such riotous ease
> That the bachelor-buttons come up with the peas.[14]

Poorman's Pleasure Garden

'Pray, how does your garden flourish? I
warrant you do not yet know the difference
betwixt a ranunculus and an anemone. God
help ye!'

WILLIAM SHENSTONE

Poorman's Pleasure Garden

By Poorman's Pleasure Garden I mean neither Ranelagh of yesterday nor Battersea of today, nor any public parks given over to twice yearly transformation scenes of tulips and dahlias.

My Poorman's Pleasure Garden may be a four-inch pot of geraniums on a town-dweller's window-sill; a green fern in a village dairy window; a hanging basket at the door of a one-up-and-one-down in the suburbs; an orange box full of wallflowers; a cat-run sown with candytufts between high brick walls; a roof-garden; a pocket-handkerchief-sized railway garden; a child's patch between the dustbin and the back door; a prison garden, or even a meat-dish, laid out with miniature rocks and trees and tiny plants, to disguise a manhole cover.

It is pleasure shared with the passer-by. This act of courtesy is by no means a new idea. Thomas Tusser, in 1580, published a list of thirty-nine different flowers for those who have no garden: 'Herbs, Branches, and Flowers, for Windows and Pots, including Batchelers buttens; Botles blew, red and tawney; Flower gentil, white and red; Flower nyce; Paunces [pansies] or Hartsease; Pragles [cowslips] greene and yellow and Velvet flowers or Frenche marigolds.'[1]

There was, in 1677, 'scarce an Ingenious Citizen that by his confinement to a Shop, being denied the priviledge of having a real Garden, but hath his boxes, pots or other receptacles for Flowers, Plants, etc. In imitation of it, what curious Representations of Banquets of Fruits, Flower pots, Gardens and such like are painted to the life to please the Eyes and satisfye the fancy of such that either cannot obtain the Felicity of enjoying them in reality, or to supply the defect that Winter annually brings?'[2]

Forty-five years later, we have this confirmation from Thomas Fairchild of the town-dweller's desire for fresh air,

sunshine and growing things. 'One may guess at the general
love my fellow citizens have for gardening in the midst of
their toil and labours by observing how much use they make
of every favourable glance of the sun to come abroad and of
furnishing their rooms or chambers with posies of flowers
and bough-pots, rather than not to have something of the
garden before them.'[3] Thomas Fairchild had a vineyard at
Hoxton, and in his will left funds for a Garden Sermon to be
preached every Whit Tuesday at St Leonard's, Shoreditch.

John Evelyn had great plans for turning cities from grey
prisons into places where families could live and breathe. He
solemnly promised to make London the healthiest, as well as
the happiest city in the world, by surrounding it with plots and
hedgerows of sweet-briar, jasmine, lilies, rosemary, lavender,
musk and marjoram. Circumstances were too strong for him.
And yet, could John Evelyn revisit his old haunts just for a
day, what would he think of our battle formation of office
blocks, with scentless rubber plants and lethal-looking
mother-in-law's tongues, stationed at the windows like
weapons at the ready? The offices are light and airy, the potted
plants are green, and it is more than three hundred years
since the plague swept London, so I suppose we have much
to be thankful for.

Washington Irving notes in his *Sketch Book* how even, 'In
the most dark and dingy quarters of the city, the drawing-
room window resembles frequently a bank of flowers.'

Flowers and plants were hawked not only in the neighbourhoods of the well-to-do, but in the dark alleys of the workers.
'Here they are! blowing, growing, all alive!' This was an old
London cry by the flower-gardeners, who wheeled the products of their small plots through the streets in a barrow,
'blowing, growing, all alive!' to tempt the purchasers in the
humble streets and alleys of working neighbourhoods. Acts of
Parliaments have put down the flower-pots which were accustomed to 'topple on the walkers' heads from the windows
of houses where-in flower fanciers dwelt.'[4]

At this time Thomas Gray was writing from Pembroke College, Cambridge, to his friend Norton Nicholls, 'and so you have a garden of your own, and you plant and transplant, and are dirty and amused; I have no such thing, you monster; nor ever shall be dirty and amused as long as I live! My gardens are in a window like those of a lodger up three pairs of stairs in Petticoat Lane or Camomile Street, and they go to bed regularly under the same roof as I do . . . dear, how charming it must be to walk out in one's own garden, and sit on a bench in the open air with a fountain and a lead statue, and a rolling stone, and an arbour.'

Even without a garden, Gray managed to get a flower or two to brighten his rooms in Southampton Row, for he wrote to Dr Wharton on 21 July 1759, 'My nosegays, from Covent Garden, consist of nothing but scarlet martagons, everlasting-peas, double stocks, pinks and flowering marjoram.'

A year earlier, Parson Woodforde, then an Oxford undergraduate, had noted in his diary these purchases; 'a New Wigg, £1. 1. 0 and two White Waistcoats,' and this charming item, 'Nosegays, £0. 0. 1.'[5]

Not everyone succumbed to the charms of pot-plants. For instance, this anonymous gentleman who wrote, 'I can endure no plants in pots – a plant in a pot is like a bird in a cage,'[6] but he was in the minority, and in the large towns there was hardly a street without its flower shop or stall, making a gay patch of colour in its shabby surroundings, with its potted geraniums, and forget-me-nots, and mignonette.

How did the poor manage to afford their little treasures of perfume and colour? Here is a scene from around St Paul's in 1851: 'Under the Piazza the costers purchase their flowers (in pots) which they exchange in the streets for old clothes. Here is ranged a small garden of flower-pots, the musk and mignonette smelling sweetly, and the scarlet geraniums, with a perfect glow of coloured air about the flowers, standing out in rich contrast with the dark green leaves of the evergreens behind them. "There's myrtles, and larels, and boxes," says one of the men selling them, "and there's a harbora witus, and lauristiners, and that bushy shrub with pink spots is heath".'[7]

Townsmen and countrymen, women and children, seem to share a desire for living colour. 'For the same reason that your town man keeps a pot of Geraniums on his window-sill . . . your countryman plants bright-coloured flowers by his door. . . . They pull as much of Heaven down as will accommodate itself to their plot of earth.'[8]

Even Leigh Hunt, whose every sentence, Alexander Smith says, 'is flavoured with the hawthorn and the primrose,' when he was imprisoned from 1813 to 1815 in Horsemonger Lane Gaol, for accurately but tactlessly describing the Prince Regent as 'a fat Adonis of fifty', was allowed to pull a bit of Heaven down for himself in his adversity. Indeed the poet Gray might have envied Hunt in his captivity. Here is Leigh Hunt's description of life in gaol, where inside he was surrounded by his books, busts, pictures and piano, while outside 'The earth I filled with flowers and young trees. There was an apple tree, from which we managed to get a pudding the second year. As to my flowers, they were allowed to be perfect. Thomas Moore, who came to see me with Lord Byron, told me he had seen no such hearts-ease . . . Here I wrote and read in fine weather sometimes under an awning. In autumn, my trellises were hung with scarlet runners, which added to the flowery investment. I used to shut my eyes in my arm chair, and affect to think myself hundreds of miles off.'[9]

On the night previous to his visit, 19 May 1813, Byron had written to Moore in anticipation,

> But now to my letter – to yours 'tis an answer –
> Tomorrow be with me, as soon as you can, sir,
> All ready and dress'd for proceeding to spunge on
> (According to compact) the wit in the dungeon –
> Pray Phoebus at length our political malice
> May not get us lodgings within the same palace![10]

Numerous charming books were published in the nineteenth century, to advise on the growing of indoor plants. Most of the books were small, in proportion to the gardens for which they were written, but they contained impressive engravings of flower-boxes covered with cork, Wardian cases of giant dimensions, and an elaborate construction known as a fern-delabrum. These were made by Mr J. Pulham of Broxbourne, 'at these works also are made pretty flower boxes, vases, and Fern-delabrum, some of these are very neatly fitted with enamelled tiles and have been greatly admired.'[11] Some of the large plant cases which stood in small cottage windows one would guess must have pampered the plants, while their owners grew spindly for lack of light. The author of *The Parlour Gardener*, claimed that the reader had only to follow his instructions, 'and his little home will become to him the Kew of his heart, and the Chatsworth of all his desires,'[11] and who could say fairer than that?

And outside, Dickens' old gentleman was busy at all seasons, 'In fine weather the old gentleman is almost constantly in the garden; and when it is too wet to go into it, he will look out of the window at it, by the hour together. He has always something to do there, and you will see him digging and sweeping and cutting and planting, with manifest delight. In spring time there is no end to the sowing of seeds, and sticking little bits of wood over them, with labels, which look like epitaphs to their memory.'[12]

Perhaps the roof garden is the most to be admired of all the Poorman's Pleasure Gardens. Cold winds, hot sun and a minimum of soil, are harsh enemies, and the gardener's attention must never flag. But if his courage does not fail, what a victory is his! 'He will tell you which day of the week the Pansy lost its second bud through the sparrows, just when it looked certain to be quite as good as the flower he got last year; or he will show you the Canariensis, baffled by the same marauders last Friday week, has tried again with a second shoot which will be out before Wednesday.'[13] And the wild life he sees in the hours spent up there among the chimney-pots — you'd never believe! 'A real honey-bee buzzing and working over the flower beds, even a spider — a real garden spider, with a shining web; a country-looking weed, a stinging nettle, — a

47

lively one that knows how to sting, and on one bright still evening, when the sunshine lingered on the gas-work's chimneys, a humming-bird hawk-moth fluttering well-pleased among the flowers.'[13]

It may be that the last of the humming-bird hawk-moths have left for more congenial climes, but since smokeless fuel zones are ever widening round our cities, at least one of the roof-gardener's enemies is routed. Soot is an older garden foe than one imagines. Even as early as 1629 Parkinson was advising his readers against situating their gardens in the vicinity of 'Lay-stalles, or common Sewers, or else near any great Brew-house, Dye-house, or any other place where there is much smoake, whether it be of straw, wood, or especially of sea-coales, which of all other is the worst, as our Citie of London can give proofe sufficient, wherein neither herbe nor tree will long prosper, nor hath done ever since the use of sea-coales beganne to bee frequent therein.'

So far, in this chapter, we have been talking of gardens measured in feet and inches, and of flowers grown singly or in mere dozens; but outside the cities, where there is space to swing a daffodil, there are gardens for travellers – neat railway gardens, and patchwork quilts of flowers tucked round old inns, and more recently, the bold borders of African marigolds and petunias that are the peace offerings of petrol stations.

In spring the railway garden is bordered with aubrieta and forget-me-nots, with here and there a clump of flowering bulbs, but these are only scene-setters for the show to come. Tidy, black-cottoned rows ending in empty seed packets impaled on small twigs, like miniature posters advertising the delights we may expect if in high summer we pass this way again, are models of weedless, finely sifted earth. Between stations the seasons come and go, scattering on the embankments primroses and violets, valerian and wild geraniums, with here and there a colony of sunflowers, montbretia, lupins, michaelmas daisies or everlasting sweet peas, escaped from the exuberant gardens of past summers.

But the warmest welcome comes from the gardens surrounding old inns. 'When travel was leisurely and ground rents were low, there was always ample space for the garden of the Chequers or the Black Lion. It supplied the inn with vegetables and the guests with nosegays. . . . In the posting houses on the great roads these pleasaunces were always kept up with some care, so that travellers might be tempted to prolong their stay.'[14]

We have come a long way from our geranium in a four-inch pot, but here for our traveller is 'the most splendid, riotous, jostling and friendly garden of them all'. This time the garden of an old coaching inn, The Basket of Roses, later to be pulled down to make way for a peculiarly bleak Parochial Hall. It is described by Compton Mackenzie in *The Passionate Elopement*.

First the landlord – the ancient man was a great gardener, as properly became a landlord whose sign was a swinging posy.

What a garden there was at the back of this florious inn. The bowling-green surrounded by four grey walls was the finest ever known, and as for the borders – deep borders twelve feet wide – they were full of every sweet flower. There were Columbines and Canterbury Bells and blue Bells of Coventry and Lilies and Candy Goldilocks with Penny flowers or White Satin and Fair Maids of France and Fair Maids of Kent and London Pride.

There was Herb of Grace and Rosemary and Lavender to pluck and crush between your fingers, while some one rolled the jack across the level green of the ground. In Spring there were Tulips and Jacynths, Dames Violets and Primroses, Cowslips of Jerusalem, Daffodils and Pansies, Lupins like spires in the dusk, and Ladies' Smocks in the shadowed corners. As for Summer, why the very heart of high June and hot July dwelt in that fragrant enclosure. Sweet Johns and Sweet Williams with Dragon flowers and crimson Peaseblossom and tumbling Peonies, Blue Moonwort and the Melancholy Gentlemen, Larksheels, Marigolds, Hearts, Hollyhocks and Candytufts. There was Venus' Looking Glass and Flower of Bristol, and Apple of Love and Blue Helmets and Herb Paris and Campion and Love in a Mist and Ladies'

49

Laces and Sweet Sultans or Turkey Cornflowers. Gilliflower Carnations (Ruffling Rob of Westminster amongst them) with Dittany and Sop in Wine and Floramer, Widow Wail and Bergamot, True Thyme and Gilded Thyme, Good Night at Noon and Flower de Luce, Golden Mouse-ear, Princes' Feathers, Pinks, and deep red Damask Roses.

It was a very wonderful garden indeed.[15]

PLATE I

May—'All A-Growing!'

Exchanging old clothes for potted plants

Etching by George Cruikshank, from *The Comic Almanack*, 1835-43.

PLATE 2

Daisy

Hand-coloured engraving by William Clark, engraver to
the London Horticultural Society, from *The Moral of
Flowers*, Mrs. Hey, 1835.

PART II

Flowers from a Cottage Garden

'Let us now come and furnish the inward parts and beds with those fine flowers that are most beseeming it: and namely Daffodils, Fritillaries, Jacinths, Saffron-flowers, Lillies, Flower-deluces, Tulipas, Anemones, French Cowslips or Beares eares, and a number of such other flowers, very beautifull, delightfull, and pleasant, whereof although many have little sweete sent to commend them, yet their earliness and exceeding varietie doth so farre countervaile that defect.'

JOHN PARKINSON

Snowdrop

Galanthus   Hope

The classic flower, the legendary snow princess, standing
aloof and pale, indifferent to her bleak surroundings; brought
as an emblem of purity to decorate the Lady Chapel on Candlemas day, 2 February, and so sometimes called Candlemas
Bells:

> The Snowdrop, in purest white arraie,
> First rears its head on Candlemasse daie.[1]

Also known as Fair Maid of February, and associated with
St Agnes day, 21 January. Content with poor soil, it cannot be
nursed or coaxed to grow where it has no mind to, but where it
has settled, it will increase and remain while generations pass.
Theophrastus mentions them growing on the hills of Greece
three hundred years before Christ.

From their first pushing through the earth they are waited
for with hope, and no one has described this pressing upwards
better than Jason Hill: 'Snowdrops fashion their leaves into
flat blades, shaped like a Roman sword, and, fitting two of
them accurately face to face, cut through the soil a way for the
flower to follow. The points of the first leaves are armed with
a hard whitish tip, very much like a small finger-nail, though
it reminds me also of the "nib" on the bill of a young chick,
with which he, too, breaks his way into the world.'[2]

One writer likens the snowdrop to a dove sent forth from
the ark to learn whether the frosts had mitigated, but Elizabeth
Barrett wrote to Robert Browning on 27 February 1845, 'To
me, unhappily, the snowdrop is much the same as the snow –
it feels as cold underfoot – and I have grown sceptical about
"the voice of the turtle", the east winds blow so loud.'

Many people dislike double snowdrops; William Morris,

53

for instance. 'Don't be swindled out of that wonder of beauty, a single snowdrop,' he said. 'There is no gain and plenty of loss in the double one.'[3] I, in my more romantic moments, regard the double snowdrop as a Sylphide among flowers, though I admit to baser thoughts, when they seem to me like buxom infants of a generation past, dressed for Sunday school and showing their drawers.

In Devonshire there was a superstition that it was unlucky to carry the first snowdrop of the year indoors. In the *Language of Flowers*, a few snowdrops in an envelope sent by a lady to a too-ardent gentleman, might be considered a polite brush-off.

Gerard had little to say about them, 'seeing that nothing is set downe hereof by the antient Writers, nor anything observed by the moderne; onely they are maintained and cherished in gardens for the beautie and rareness of the floures, and sweetness of their smell.'

They have a faint perfume, it is true, but it seems to come from afar, like the horns of elfland faintly blowing. It is one with the aloofness and frigidity of the flower.

That the adventurous and early bee has a liking for them is evident. 'The snowdrops shone whitely this morning like snow in an unnaturally hard and good preservation in summer sunshine; an adventurous bee hummed and industriously sucked what one felt must be cold comfort from the snowdrop. I could not help wondering whether such clay-cold flowers really had any honey, but the perseverance of the bees — for now there were at least two, or even three, — was strong evidence.'[4]

> In the pale sunshine, with frail wings unfurled,
> Comes to the bending snowdrop the first bee.
> She gives her winter honey prudently;
> And faint with travel in a bitter world,
> The bee makes music, tentative and low,
> And spring awakes and laughs across the snow.[5]

That this chill-veined flower should cleave its way through bitter earth with its raised spear before the final rout of winter, when it might just as well wait until the sunshine has warmed and softened the soil for easier birth is only one of nature's miracles.

> Now, now, as low I stooped, thought I,
> I will see what this snowdrop IS;
> So shall I put much argument by,
> And solve a lifetime's mysteries.[6]

Crocus

The candle flames of the crocus light the way back to the
ancient world, for they broke out round the feet of the blinded
Oedipus as he groped his way back to Colonna. They adorned
the marriage beds of the Greeks, and took their name from the
beautiful youth, the lover of Smilax, who at his untimely death
took in exchange their form.

To the old writers all crocuses and colchicums were included under the name of saffron; but it was the real saffron
crocus, *C. sativus*, which was collected nearly four thousand
years ago and used for spices, perfumes and dyes. The dried
stigmas and part of the style of two thousand flowers went into
one ounce of dye.

To the Greeks it was a royal flower, and it was strewn in
theatres, courts and private houses. Perfumes were made of it,
which were sprayed over the guests from small fountains. In
the Palace of Knossos there is a painting of a youth gathering
saffron flowers. In Rome Nero regarded it as a potent love-
potion, and it was sprinkled in the streets when he made his
royal progress through the city.

In ancient Ireland a king's mantle was dyed with saffron,
and saffron-dyed shirts were worn by people of rank in the
Hebrides. In medieval illuminations it was used as a glaze over
tin foil as a substitute for gold. The large sum of seven pounds
and eight shillings was paid by the Monastery of Durham in
1539 for six and a half pounds of crocus; evidently a greater
quantity than the monks could grow in their own apothecary's
garden.

As a drug it was believed to have cheering powers and when
a man was in high spirits he was said to have slept on a bag of
saffron. Gerard speaks of it as making 'the sences more quicke

and lively, shaketh off heavie and drowsie sleepe, and making
a man mery'. Gerard grew six sorts of crocus in his garden in
Holborn, among them *C. aureous*. 'It hath floures of a most
perfect shining yellow colour, seeming afar off to be a hot
glowing cole of fire. That pleasing plant was sent to me from
Robinus of Paris, that painful and curious searcher for
simples.' Gerard probably also grew *C. vernus*, the forbear of
all the large purple and white crocuses of today, which escaped
from gardens and naturalized in the fields outside Nottingham.

Richard Hakluyt, the geographer, wrote in 1589 that the
saffron crocus was introduced into England from Tripoli in
1339 by a pilgrim who hid a corm in his hollowed palmer's
staff: 'And so he brought the root into this realme, with venture
of his life, for if he had bene taken by the law of the country
from whence it came he had died for the fact.'[1]

Other writers claim that it was mentioned in an English
herbal of the tenth century, but disappeared and was re-intro-
duced by the returning crusaders. King Henry I, it is said,
valued it greatly as a spice, and forbade the ladies of his court
to use up his supplies to dye their hair. This story casts
doubts upon the claims of Hakluyt's resourceful pilgrim, but
at whatever date and by whatever means, it was cultivated in
Saffron Walden by men called 'crokers', and thus it was that
the three crocus flowers in the arms of Saffron Walden
originated. Women were employed to gather the flowers just
before they opened, and they then carried them home and
removed the stamens.

James I thought much of its herbal properties as a cure for
measles and other rashes. Queen Caroline, having read her
Gerard's *Herball* carefully, no doubt, put saffron in her tea to
cure depression; and perhaps to make them 'mery', saffron was
sold in the bird-shops of St Martin's Lane to be given to
moulting canaries.

In Switzerland it was used in the same way and for the same
purpose as peony roots were used, and hung round the necks
of children to ward off the evil eye. So highly was it regarded

57

in Europe, that in Nuremberg in the fifteenth century, men who sold adulterated saffron were buried alive, or burned in the market place with their adulterated wares.

But belief in its powers as a love potion waned; laundresses found finer starch and better dyes; and more reliable cures for depression were sought if not found, until by the early nineteenth century saffron was cultivated for colouring and flavouring only, in a few small villages in Essex. It is still used to flavour and colour rice in Spain and Persia, and *bouillabaisse*, the fish stew, so popular on the Mediterranean coast, but in English cookery it is little used except in the Cornish saffron cake.

Although a rarer pleasure now, still the autumn crocuses surprise us when we have forgotten their very existence; and still we await the crocuses of spring, like Byron's Assyrians 'gleaming in purple and gold,' or D. H. Lawrence's lilac-coloured Tuscan army, 'like an ennumerable encampment. You may see them at twilight with all the buds shut, in the mysterious stillness of the grassy underworld, palely glimmering like myriad folded tents,' until gradually 'they begin to lower their tents and abandon camp.'[2]

E.V.B. described these delicately-sturdy flowers under the frost. 'It certainly is the prettiest sight imaginable, these Crocuses thrown lightly, as it were, upon the frosted turf in garlands of amethyst and amber. The rime, covering up all varied greens and browns of earth and grass with a veil of pearly grey, gives a most pure and charming result. If you look quite near . . . the flowers seem all dipped in pounded sugar.'[3]

But to a four-year-old child they were so unforgettably beautiful, that Harriet Martineau could write in later life, 'My idea of Heaven was of a place gay with yellow and blue crocuses'.[4]

Daffodil

Narcissus   Chivalry

There is a tradition that England's first daffodil was brought
to our shores by some Venetian ship, but whether the wild
daffodil, the Lent lily, is a true native or not, it still blows its
little golden trumpet in our woods and copses, although its
music diminishes year by year. Clusius wrote in the sixteenth
century that daffodils grew in such profusion in the meadows
near Cheapside that all the taverns and shops were decked out
with them, and Gerard said, 'It is not greatly to our purpose,
particularly to seek out their places of growing wilde, seeing
we have them all and everie one of them in our London
gardens in great abundance.' Market women sold them in the
streets, and the gardens of town and country were bright with
them in spring.

At the beginning of this century Dion Clayton Calthrop
wrote, 'There are those who carry enormous baskets on their
heads, and cry in some incomprehensible tongue words
intended to convey a message such as "All fresh". To see a
gorgeous glowing mass of Daffodils sway down the street
borne triumphantly aloft like the litter of some Princess is one
of those sights to repay many grey days.'[1] Today, wild daffodils
are still sold in the streets by the gipsies at Easter time, thus
presenting me with a serious moral problem. Shall I walk by
on the other side and discourage these lawless folk in their evil
practices, or, since the flowers are already picked or uprooted
and will only die if no one buys them, shall I weaken and buy?
I weaken and buy.

It was not only for money that daffodils were sold. In
Lancashire the children of the poor sold bunches of Lent
lilies for pins, this lost currency of a bygone age. It is strange
to think that within living memory pins were given as change

59

in draper's shops in lieu of a farthing; and pins were paid by kind-hearted relatives and friends to see a peepshow of flower petals beneath glass and viewed through a small window cut in the brown paper that covered it. But whether in exchange for pins or new pence, each year the wild daffodils grow fewer, and even in 1920 Canon Vaughan was writing, 'In former days the daffodil seems to have been much commoner than it is now . . . it is curious to notice how partial the plant is to the neighbourhood of monastic ruins. No doubt the good brethren who were lovers of the beautiful delighted in its presence and encouraged the bulbs to spread near their sacred surroundings . . . that the plant is commonly associated with the lily tribe is clear from its popular name of Lent Lily, which in the Isle of Wight is sometimes corrupted into Lantern Lily.'[2]

So many poets have written of the daffodil, but it will always remain Wordsworth's own, and although his poem is too well-known for inclusion here, less well-known but not less vivid is his sister Dorothy's description. 'They grew among the mossy stones; — some rested their heads on these stones as on a pillow, the rest tossed and reeled and danced, and seemed as if they verily laughed with the wind they looked so gay and glancing.'[3]

> O yellow flowers by Herrick sung,
> O yellow flowers that danced and swung
> In Wordsworth's verse, and now to me,
> Unworthy, from this pleasant lea,
> Laugh back, unchanged and ever young.[4]

No wonder they were called Lent lilies. Here is Francis Kilvert's entry in his diary for the first Sunday in Lent, 10 April 1878. 'I went to Church in a fly with Mary who rode in great state and pride. The morning sun was shining fair and bright as we walked up the path to the Church. There was a sweet stillness and Sunday peace upon everything. Multitudes of daffodils grew about the Church, shining in the bright spring sunlight. I never saw daffodils in such numbers or so beautiful. They grew in forests, multitudes and multitudes, about the park and under the great elms, most of them in full blossom. As we went in we saw fresh groups of daffodils under the trees, golden gleam after golden gleam in the sweet sunshine. It was quite dazzling.'

In 1970 the bi-centenary of Wordsworth's birth took place in Cockermouth and the local children played an important part in the ceremony. Each child gave and planted a single daffodil bulb in his memory, and later every child carried three flowers to place at the foot of a bust of the poet which was un-veiled by his great-great-grandson.

The flower customs of Britain are disappearing with the wild daffodils, but Daffodil Sunday, the first Sunday in April, which was celebrated in the village of Dymock, ten miles from Gloucester, by the gathering of daffodils for the London hospitals, we should do well to keep. And France would do well to keep her Grande Jeannette, the daffodil egg which was sold in the streets of Paris at Easter time. Colette, to whom flowers and animals were 'people,' described it:

'This Jeannette is always thirsty. With the aid of its tender yet crisp green tube, it drinks as though through a straw. . . . From its neck flutters a ruffled slip of silk. Oh, this Jeannette, no one has ever been able to teach it to tie its cravat correctly! This does not prevent it from being the one and only bloom favoured by Parisian florists when, for the Easter festival, they make huge eggs of it and distribute them by the cartload through the streets. The florist plants a plume of spiky green leaves at the small end of the egg. No one knows why, but tradition demands it. It requires little more for the Jeannette egg to become a pineapple.'[5]

The daffodil receives more visitors than any other wild flower in our islands; visitors to the Lake District, to the daffodil fields of Gloucestershire, and to the picturesque Isle of Menteith, where the young Mary, Queen of Scots planted daffodil bulbs whose descendants are still growing there. Flower and seed and root form an endless chain back into history, and a leaf in the hand may, if we but knew it, bridge nearly three hundred years to a leaf on a bush in Addison's garden, as he sits writing his article for the *Tatler*. 'There is not a bush in blossom within a mile of me, which I am not acquainted with, nor scarce a daffodil or cowslip that withers away in my neighbourhood without my missing it.'[6]

The Lent lily may have been an unrecorded witness to many a battle fought on British soil, but in John Masefield's verse drama, *The Daffodil Fields*, the grim combat between two men who love the same woman is fought before the back-cloth of the recurring seasons of the wild daffodils, until the death of both brings to an end 'this old tale of woe among the daffodils'.

So many writers I should have liked to include; Ben Jonson, Herrick, Keats, Humbert Wolfe, W. H. Davies and Vita Sackville-West among them, but we must leave room for other flowers and so here, to end, is a haunting little verse from Oscar Wilde,

> There is a tiny yellow daffodil,
>   The butterfly can see it from afar,
> Although one summer evening's dew could fill
>   Its little cup twice over, ere the star
> Had called the lazy shepherd to his fold,
>   And be no prodigal.[7]

Tulip

Tulipa   Imagination and dreaminess

So much has been written of the tulip as a gamblers' flower, when Tulipomania swept Holland and brought that usually sober and hard-headed nation to the edge of disaster, that there can be nothing to add. That storm of speculative horticultural madness reached this country in diminished force in the eighteenth century when it quietly died, and the tulip as a money-symbol was forgotten, and it was valued once again as a beautiful and long-lasting flower. May she rest in peace.

HERE LIES BURIED

A

ROSE COLOURED TULIP

WHO CAME ACROSS THE SEAS

FROM THE KINGDOM OF

HOLLAND

UNDER THIS EARTH

SHE

AND ONE HUNDRED OF HER SISTERS

ARE WAITING FOR THE SPRING

WHEN THEY WILL UNFOLD THEMSELVES

FROM THEIR LONG SLEEP AND ADORN

WITH THEIR PLEASANT FACES THE SOUTH

BORDER FACING THE STUDY WINDOW.[1]

It is altogether more satisfying to regard the tulip as an artists' flower, and as a gardeners' flower.

As an artists' flower, its formal grace has appealed to the designers of pottery, metal work and embroidery throughout the centuries. About fifty years ago the collecting of pottery and porcelain tulips became widely popular, and at least one

West End dealer specialized in them. They were produced at Coalport, Rockingham and Derby, and there were quite a number of Staffordshire china and earthenware examples. Tulip candlesticks were charming, and a set of tulip custard cups was, even then, a rarity. The tulip also played an important part in the regular and stylized patterns of Persian carpets. It appeared in splendid profusion in the flower paintings of seventeenth- and eighteenth-century Dutch art, and there was scarcely a flower painting by Breughel, Bosschaert, Savery or Ruysch in which at least one fantastically striped or feathered tulip does not loll unseasonably with the flowers of summer and autumn, as if the artist could not bear to leave them out. In Turkish art, also, it so predominated in floral designs during the reign of Sultan Ahmed III that the age became known as the 'tulip' period.

Interest in this adaptable flower was revived when it caught the imagination of the world of Art Nouveau, and instead of the rich downward curves of the Dutch painters, it lifted a slender head upward on a tall straight stem from bottom to top of a printed page, or filled the elongated spaces of clouded glass vases or polished brass door plates.

Until recent years flowers have coloured the pages of poetry and romance, and of travel books too, but few have provided the principal character, as well as the title, of a novel. *The Black Tulip*, written by the elder Dumas, is an exciting romance, complete with hero, heroine and black-hearted villain, about the breeding and subsequent adventures of the first black tulip, until its final triumphant festival in Haarlem when 'one could see, in the midst of the peaceful and perfumed train, the black tulip, borne on a litter covered with white velvet fringed with gold'.

Strangely enough, the tulip played its modest part in the Second World War in occupied Holland and also in Paris, where they were eaten as vegetables. The novelist Colette wrote of her war-time memories: 'There was a time when fashion and frenzied speculation required you to be black, and very high prices were paid for you. The deeper your mourning mauve became, the more your worshippers ruined themselves on your account. But came a time of famine, and your precious bulbs were cooked and eaten. In more recent days you served a noble purpose: during the bad springs of the Occupation, in a Paris swollen with hope and embittered by deep resentment, the florists would sell bulbs, three to a pot, which found a way of spreading sedition. "A pretty pot of tulips, Madame, to grow in the home?" March came, and as the pearly bulbs awakened, splitting their dry-skinned envelopes, they brought forth, in place of tulips, three sprightly ultrapatriotic hyacinths – one blue, one white, one red.'[2]

In the nineteen-thirties a competition was set by Sylvia Lynd in the *Week-end Review*, in which competitors had to name and describe six supposedly new tulip bulbs after six famous men of the time. The second-prize winner took verbatim descriptions from a genuine catalogue, and applied them with witty precision. Here are two of them:

Mussolini. The blackest of all tulips. Large, erect, carried on a stiff stem. Grand forcer.

Dean Inge. Mauve, shaded purple, of good form, having an azure-blue halo. Effective in lawns and terraces. Very chaste.

And now, the gardeners' flower. An instructive conversation between the Chevalier and the Countess, in one of those polite little books which so often imparted knowledge by way of conversation; a Gardening Without Tears.

CHEVALIER: What may be the Use of the little moveable Tent which I have frequently observed in the Gardens of the Curious?

COUNTESS: It is placed on a Bed of fine Tulips, and either raised or lowered in such a Manner as may be most proper to shelter the flowers from melted Snows which sully their Lustre.[3]

And this, from *The Garden Book* of Thomas Hanmer, although I think this is carrying things altogether too far. 'I know in Paris one of the ablest florists there, who had got a great deal of money by Tulipes, and hee assured mee hee chang'd his habitation purposely every third or fowerth yeare in Paris because of his Tulipes, which he found infinitely better'd by varietyes of aire as well as Earth.'[4]

And next we share the enthusiasm known to all good gardeners in May, even though we do not all provide ourselves with little sticks to prove it. 'And now the florists fly about to see and examine and take the chiefe pleasure of Gardens, admiring the new varietyes that Spring produces, and being impatient of delays open the very buttons scarce yet coloured, but with a little sticke or two for the purpose, lest they should prejudice them with the touch of their fingers.'[4]

Our early garden tulips were mostly cultivated from *T. gesneria*, which was brought to Vienna by the Viennese ambassador to Suleiman the Magnificent, Augerius Busbecq. The first illustration of a tulip appears in 1561, in the herbal of Conrad von Gesner, after whom the species was called. Once we had a small wild tulip of our own, which grew in the valley of the Don, near Doncaster, and in the meadows outside Nottingham.

'It gives pleasure to me, a true lover as I am of my own country to know, that we are neither indebted to Turks nor turbans* for the origin of this splendid wild flower, which was, no doubt, more plentiful in the days of our Elizabethan poets, and which is mentioned in Ben Jonson's *Pan's Anniversary*, by the very name it still bears.'[5]

But Maund, whose beautiful *Botanic Garden* is a collector's prize, is slightly on the defensive. 'We are fully sensible that if measured by the florists' rules of beauty, our present unchangeable Tulip (*Tulipa Sylvestris*) will stand excluded of their society; but none would estimate an Italian beauty and a Dutch Burgomaster by the same standard of value.'

But not everyone shares this enthusiasm. 'I knew a man who had always been happy until the moment when some one sent him a present of a dozen tulip roots. I never saw but one man

---

*'tulipa' comes from 'turban' in Turkish.

Tulips.

Pl:34.

The Changeable Tulip

The Bleeding Tulip

The Golden Tulip

The Pearl & Crimson
Tulip

The Auriflame, or Gold
and Scarlet Tulip

The White & Purple Tulip

PLATE 3

Tulips

Engraving. Van Huysum pinxt. J. Hill sculp. From *Eden:
or, A Compleat Body of Gardening*, 'Sir' John Hill, 1762.

PLATE 4

Daffodils, Irises, Amaryllis

Engraving, unsigned. From *Eden: or, a Compleat Body of Gardening*, 'Sir' John Hill, 1762.

more embarrassed, and that was a merchant of Marseilles, to whom an African prince sent two tigers and a panther, begging him to keep them for his sake.'[6] I suppose it was the prospect of being thrust willy-nilly into the world of high finance which so disturbed him.

Here is another rather acid bit of dialogue between the inevitable fair lady and her gardener.

BELAURA: But what's the wit, prithee, of yonder tulip?
GEORGIO: You may read there the wit of a young courtier;
Pride, and show of colours, a fair promising,
Deare when 'tis bought, and quickly comes to nothing.[7]

But let us leave these critics and return to that rare black tulip, and the school of tulip growers who founded their faith on the belief that

To despise flowers is to offend God;
The more beautiful the flower is,
the more is God offended by contempt of it;
Therefore he who despises the tulip,
offends God exceedingly,[8]

and rather than offending God, even a little, let us agree that 'there is no Lady or Gentleman of any worth that is not caught with this delight.'[9]

Primrose

Primula   Young love

In spite of the meaning in the *Language of Flowers* there is
something spinsterish about the primrose. Perhaps it is the
name, or maybe its pale colour and that greenish eye that gives
it such a strait-laced look. True its wrinkled leaves have a hint
of the damp hands of housewives and Monday wash-days in
generations past, more suggestive of the mother of a large
family; but the flower keeps that deceptive frail appearance,
like an ailing spinster far tougher than she would have you
believe. Shakespeare must have thought so too, for he called
them 'pale primroses that die unmarried.'[1]

But Mary Webb suspected their virginity. Transplanted
from woods to garden, like foolish country lasses lured to the
big city,

> My primroses,
> That gave a greenish, pale moonshine,
> O mischief-making bees!
> Are red as wine.[2]

Flower alike of country lane and cottage garden, the primrose sends its yellow invitations out to us to visit the country
before spring is ready to greet us there, and if we are too
occupied with urban things then gipsies come and stand at
street corners, offering small bunches tied with wool to remind
us.

It is the commuters' flower; it climbs the banks of railway
cuttings and forces us to look up from our crosswords and
remember that the days are beginning to draw out. Most of us
have read about the Bluebell Line, and some have even
travelled on it, but not so many know about the Primrose Line
from Victoria to Brighton.

Crowding the embankment
In sunshine and in rain,
A hundred thousand primroses
Are waiting for a train.

From Balcombe down to Wivelsfield
So wan they look and frail,
And hoping for a holiday
By means of British Rail.

How pleasant for the porters,
How glad the guard would be
If a hundred thousand primroses
Went riding to the sea.

It is the gardener's flower too, and in spite of all the rare
and beautiful things that he must have grown in his long life-
time, it is Fred Streeter's favourite. A big cake was iced for his
ninetieth birthday, and decorated with primroses. 'I defy
anyone to remain mumpish and groovy or fanatical in a room
full of Primroses,'[3] said Reginald Farrer, another famous
plantsman.

It is also the politician's flower, Disraeli's flower. 'The
gems and jewels of nature,' he called them, 'the ambassadors
of spring . . . of all flowers, the one that retains its beauty
longest.' Queen Victoria made her first gift of spring flowers
to Disraeli in 1875, when she learnt that the primrose was his
favourite. Her last arrived just before he died, with the
accompanying message, 'Dearest Lord Beaconsfield, I send
you a few of your favourite spring flowers'. There was one
more. A large wreath of primroses arrived from the old
Queen to the dead statesman. In 1883 the Primrose League
was founded, with much hearty singing of the League's song:

Oh come, ye Tories, all unite
To bear the Primrose badge with might,
And work and hope and strive and fight,
And may God defend the right.

69

Primrose day in Victorian London was always enjoyable.

> Make me a song of Primrose Day;
> Along the streets of London Town
> A Primrose snowstorm settles down
> And makes each street an amber way[4]

It is almost unbelievable that there could be anyone living in Europe who did not know the primrose, yet Elizabeth, enjoying her German garden in 1898, wrote of her German friend Irais, 'She had heard so much about primroses, and they have got so mixed up in her mind with leagues and dames, and Disraelis, that she longs to see this political flower.'[5]

Dorothy Wordsworth, when she was living in Grasmere, wrote in her journal on Tuesday, 11 January 1803, 'We stopped our horse close to the hedge, opposite a tuft of primroses, three flowers in full blossom and a bud. They reared themselves up among the green moss. We debated long whether we should pluck [them], and at last left them to live out their day, which I was right glad of at my return the Sunday following, for there they remained, uninjured either by cold or wet.'

A century later, W. H. Davies might have been describing Dorothy's primrose family:

> The first born is full blown and tall;
> Two in half bloom just reach his chin,
> Three buds are small,

a family group in miniature.

A pale yellow ointment, called spring salve, was made in country houses, both large and small, which was used for removing tan and freckles. 'Of the leaves of Primroses is made as fine a salve to heal wounds as any that I know; you shall be taught to make salves of any herb at the latter end of the book', says Culpeper in his herbal, and adds, 'make this as you are taught there, and do not (you that have any ingenuity in you) see your poor neighbours go with wounded limbs when a halfpenny cost will heal them.'

Keats wrote to John Hamilton Reynolds from the Isle of Wight on 17 April 1817, 'As for primroses, the Island ought to be called Primrose Island — that is, if the nation of Cowslips agree thereto, of which there are divers Clans just beginning to lift up their heads.'

Perhaps, in spite of leagues and dames, Disraelis and commuters, they are really holiday flowers, as Izaak Walton thought. 'When I sat last on this primrose bank, and looked down on the meadows, I thought of them, as Charles the Emperor did of Florence, that they were too pleasant to be looked on, but only on holidays.'[6]

Polyanthus

Imagine a bunch of primroses on one stalk dressed for a fancy dress party, and you have a polyanthus. No more richly coloured, sweetly scented, well-tempered flower exists, as the Lancashire and Scottish weavers knew. Born of humble parentage, like the men who bred them, this truly British flower, a hybrid of the primrose and the oxlip, brought a richness into the garden that its parents never knew.

There seems to be no mention of it before 1564, but during the next hundred years many gardeners busied themselves in its culture, and the finest flowers fetched as much as one guinea a root, a high price in those days. Many of the loveliest came from Ireland, where soil and climate provide all that the family requires.

They grow in a wide range of colours; white, yellow, pink, peach, bronze, lilac, crimson, purple, scarlet and mahogany. They may be single, double or frilled, but the beautiful laced varieties bred for show, have almost disappeared. In their heyday in the seventeenth and eighteenth centuries when they were cultivated with great care and patience by the artisan-florists, they answered to such splendid names as Darlington's Defiance, Fillingham's Tantararara, Mason's Black Prince, Eckersley's Jolly Dragoon and Heapey's Smiler. Could anyone resist Heapey's Smiler?

In contrast to these splendid characters we have a sort of Harlequinade of queer primrose oddities; the Jack-in-the-Green, the Hose-in-Hose, Jackanapes, and Galligaskin. Each has his own well-defined characteristics, as Harlequin differs from Joey the Clown, and Pantaloon from either. They have now become collectors' flowers, and never were the strange sports of any flowers so well worth collecting. Some that were described by the old garden writers have gone forever; some may still be obtained, but are only to be found in specialists' catalogues. Many, no doubt, still grow in cottage gardens, or may turn up accidentally here and there.

Jack-in-the-Green, which was extensively cultivated about 1600, wears a Tudor ruff of green beneath the bloom, which may be of any colour. It was also called Jack-in-the-Pulpit.

Hose-in-Hose has one bloom arising out of another, like Tudor stockings. Each bloom is of the same colour as its fellow.

Jackanapes is similar to Hose-in-Hose, but it wears green stripes on each ruff.

Jackanapes-on-Horseback is in much the same form, but it carries a tuft of coloured leaves beneath the bloom. Parkinson says that the country people called this the Franticke, Fantasticke, or Foolish Cowslip. 'We have in our gardens another kinde, not much differing in leaves from the former Cowslip, and it is called Fantasticke or Foolish, because it beareth at the toppe of the stalke a bush or tufte of small long greene leaves, with some yellow leaves, as it were peeces of flowers broken, and standing among those greene leaves. And sometimes some stalkes among those greene leaves at the toppe (which are a little larger than when it hath but broken peeces of flowers) doe carry whole flowers in huskes like the single kind.'

Galligaskin has an enlarged calyx and a frilled ruff underneath the bloom, but it is a single flower. It was 'crumpled on the sides of the huskes, which do somewhat resemble mens hose that they did wear, and took the name of Gallegaskins from thence.' Parkinson called it the Curl'd Cowslip.

Sacheverell Sitwell is an enthusiastic collector of the old polyanthus and its related curiosities. To read the chapter on 'The Old Primrose and Polyanthus' in his book, *Old Fashioned Flowers*, is to combine a visit to the Harlequinade and Pantomime, with a look at a Diaghilev ballet, and a few fairground sideshows for good measure.

73

Cowslip

Cowslips, first cousins of the primroses, and probable ancestors of the polyanthus, bear a strong resemblance to their relatives, but like the members of other families, each has its own particular characteristics, and prefers to live apart. The primrose likes semi-concealment among woods and copses; the polyanthus is a garden dweller, but the cowslip prefers to sun itself in open fields.

Izaak Walton loved the plant: '– when the lawyer is swallowed up in business, and the statesman in preventing or contriving plots, then we sit on cowslip-banks, hear the birds sing, and possess ourselves in as much quietness as these silent silver streams, as we now see glide so quietly by us.'[1] This venerable fisherman made practical use of his cowslip bank, for he had a recipe for frying his catch in 'peeped' cowslips, that is, the yellow corolla, pulled from its calyx.

This is a plant of many regional names; it was Fairy Cups in Lincolnshire; Crewells in Dorsetshire; Cowstripling in Yorkshire; Horsebuckle in Kent; Herb Peter or St Peter's Keys, which became in time, Peterkeys or Peterkin; Our Lady's Keys; Paigle, Paggle or Pea Gulls; and nicest of all, Cuckooboots. Parkinson gives us other names that are no longer heard, but may be found buried in the dusty pages of old herbals. 'In some Countries they call them Paigles, or Palsieworts, or Petty Mulleins, which are called Cowslips in others.'

It was known as Palsiewort because it was used as a cure for palsie. Cowslip, from the Saxon word cuslippe, was from a supposed likeness of its perfume to the breath of cows, but the Cold Comfort Farm school of thought will have none of that, and say that it is because it flourishes best in cows' slop or cow droppings.

74

Cowslips were first described as garden flowers by Turner in *A New Herball*. 'There are some grene cowislippes and some dubble, tripel, quadrupel, that grow in gardines.'[2]

They were also mentioned in Lyte's *Herball*, 1578, as garden plants. Parkinson says that they are plentiful in the fields but many take delight in them and plant them in their garden; but by the beginning of the eighteenth century the cowslip was out of fashion as a garden plant, having given way to the larger and showier polyanthus. Today it remains a much-loved, ever-scarcer wild flower, but is seldom seen in gardens.

Cowslips were considered very necessary in the stillroom. 'Of the juice or the water of the flowers of Cowslips, divers Gentlewomen know how to cleanse the skin from spots or discolourings therein, as also to take away the wrinkles thereof and cause the skin to become smooth and faire.'[3]

Culpeper offered some practical advice. 'Our city dames know well enough the ointment or distilled water of it adds beauty, or at least restores it when it is lost . . . if the flowers be not well dried, and kept in a warm place, they will soon putrefy and look green: Have a special eye over them. If you let them see the Sun once a month, it will do neither the Sun nor them harm.' This was in spite of scathing denunciation by Dr Turner, Dean of Wells, who in 1551 had written, 'Some women sprinkle ye floures of cowslip wt whyte wine, and after still it and wash their faces wt that water, to drive wrinkles away and to make them fayre in the eyes of the worlde rather than in the eyes of God, Whom they are not afrayde to offend.'[2]

Perhaps the reverend gentleman would have considered the flowers more usefully employed in the making of cowslip wine, for it was said that whoever had tasted Buckinghamshire cowslip wine would have no desire for the choicest vintage of France. Or might he have sipped a less potent cup of cowslip tea, still enjoyed by country folk at the beginning of this century? This was made by picking the golden pips from a handful of cowslips, pouring boiling water over them, and letting the tea stand a few minutes to infuse. It could be drunk either with or without sugar as preferred. The tea sounds pleasant enough, but Granny Wallon's cowslip wine must have been a heady brew. 'The wine in the cups was still and golden, transparent as a pale spring morning. It smelt of ripe grass in some far-away field and its taste was as delicate as air. It seemed so innocent, we would swig away happily and even the youngest guzzled it down. Then a curious rocking would seize the head; tides rose from our feet like a fever, the kitchen walls began to shudder and shift, and we all fell in love with each other.'[4]

But a cup of instant cowslip tea, that cheers but not inebriates, evidently had little effect: 'It was such a treat to brew tea for ourselves, that we always sat down to our feast with great delight; but we found it difficult to finish the beverage when we had drunk a little of it'. Cowslip wine mixed with the same quantity of water 'was a great solace to us during the measles. . . . In the neighbourhood of Ripon there are old women who make it a profession for the season to collect Cowslips, pick off the corollas, and offer the articles for sale. The price for the corollas, or, in technical language, "the pips", is 1s. 6d. per peck.'[5]

Children made their own version of cowslip tea 'by getting a bottle, putting in as much sugar as their mothers would allow them . . . then cowslip "peeps" . . . filling up with water, well shaking, and then ready for sale. It is generally vended at one pin per spoonful, but should the market be over-stocked, sales are effected at all kinds of prices, and stocks often fall as low as three spoonfuls per pin.'[6] Margaret Plues' childhood memories of cowslip wine make even measles seem worth while; but perhaps the greatest joy to children were the cowslip balls, called tisty-tosties, made by tying the stalks together and pulling down the blossoms to cover the stems. What lovely golden scented balls they were, playthings fit for a princess. Prue Sarn, in *Precious Bane*, remembered them. 'It was a wonderful thing to see our meadows at Sarn when the cowslip was in blow. Gold-over they were, so that you would think not even an angel's feet were good enough to walk them.

You could make a tossy ball before a thrush had gone over his song twice, for you'd only got to sit down and gather with both hands.'[7]

These golden balls were also used as lover-diviners. Tossing them from hand to hand, young girls would sing, 'Tisty, tosty, tell me true, Who shall I be married to?' followed by the names of all the eligible bachelors in the neighbourhood. When the ball dropped, the name last mentioned was that of the future husband.

Cowslips, like buttercups and daisies, are true children's flowers. 'The children seemed to be trying to gather all the flowers. It was their way of striving to grasp the infinite. They were scattered over the hillside, where the pale sward was made an airy or liquid substance by the innumerable cowslips nodding upon its surface, as upon a lake, that held their small shadows each quite clear. All day they gathered flowers, and threw them away, and gathered more, and still they were no less. The earth continued to murmur with blissful ease, as if like the wandering humble-bee, it were drowsed with the warmth and the abundance. One child separated herself from the rest . . . and looked steadily for a moment at the whole of earth and sky, and grew solemn, only to return to the other pleasure of the hundred cowslips just at her feet, the crystal and emerald wings among them, the pearly snails, the daisies, and the chips of chalk like daisies.'[8]

But Edward Thomas's children are children no more, and never again will English children be wild-flower millionaires, for now they must be taught to conserve and guard their fast-disappearing treasures.

Poor John Clare wrote sadly to the cowslip:

> But I'm no more akin to thee,
> A partner of the spring;
> For time has had a hand with me,
> And left an alter'd thing.

To George Ryland a cowslip field meant a haven to the returned traveller:

Here was I born and here I lie
In the quiet of the cowslip fields:
I chafed at the blue unchanging sky
And the quiet of the cowslip fields.
So I sought my fortune beyond the seas
And toiled and travelled and lived at ease
And cheated and begged and starved, and I
Came back to the blue unchanging sky
And the quiet of the cowslip fields.[9]

But Richard Church has described these pure and gentle flowers more delicately and accurately perhaps than any other poet. He calls them 'a sort of embodiment of the genius of Botticelli'.[10]

Auricula

The auricula's place in the Poorman's Nosegay is assured, for John Claudius Loudon, the great Victorian horticultural writer, husband of the equally famous Jane Loudon, wrote, 'It is like the Tulip, Pink, etc., a poor man's flower, and a fine blow is rarely seen in the gardens of the nobility and gentry.'[1]

This younger relative of the primrose and polyanthus grew wild in the Alps, from where the Flemish gardeners first procured it. In its native district the roots were eaten to prevent giddiness. In other parts of the world the apothecaries grew it in their gardens as a remedy for palsy, and called it Paralytica.

It was brought to England by the Huguenots when they were driven out after the Massacre of St Bartholomew in 1572, and became the favourite flower in Lancashire, where so many of the refugees settled. Known as Bear's Ears, from the shape of their leaves, the word became corrupted to Baziers in the north of England, and there was an old song still being sung at the end of the nineteenth century that went,

> Come listen awhile to what we shall say
> Concerning the season, the season of May;
> For the flowers they are springing, the little birds singing,
> And the baziers are sweet in the mornings of May.

From Lancashire most of the London florists were supplied, until as so often happened with other flowers, the Dutch captured the market and sold us the offspring of our own flowers. In the eighteenth century a rare auricula could fetch as much as £20, and so great was the perfection to which this plant was brought, that a gardener of Colchester, by the name of Henry

Stove, had some plants with a hundred and thirty-three blossoms on one stem. Striped auriculas were bred, and many beauties that have been lost to cultivation and may now only be seen in old flower paintings and prints. John Rea in 1665 mentioned the purple and yellow striped auricula of Mistris Buggs.

Thomas Hanmer grew auriculas in his garden in Bettisfield. 'The sorts of this Flower are not to bee number'd, nor the colours of all of them to bee fittly named or described. Wee have White, Yellowes of all sorts, Haire colours, Orenges, Cherry colours, Crimson and other Redds, Violetts, PURPLES, MURREYS [mulberry], TAWNEYS, OLIVES, CINNAMON Colours, ASH colour, DUNNS and what not? but wee esteeme most such as have great and white eyes in the middle of the flowers, and most flowers on a stalke, if it bee strong and high. Faire Yellow Eyes are also good, and generally such Eyes as endure raine best, and are longest in washing away. . . . Diverse of the Hairecolours, or LEATHER COATES, as they are usually tearm'd, have had names impos'd upon them as TUGGEYS, LANCYES, LOOKERS, HUMFREYS, and other Leathercoates.'[2]

At Ranelagh in 1749, when Horace Walpole described the illuminations, 'The amphitheatre was illuminated; and in the middle was a circular bower, composed of all kinds of firs in tubs, from twenty to thirty feet high: under them orange-trees, with small lamps in each orange, and below them all sorts of the finest auriculas in pots; and festoons of natural flowers hanging from tree to tree.' Those were the days.

By the nineteenth century much was written about the cultivation of auriculas, and many fascinating names were listed; such as Buckley's Jolly Tar, Clough's Do-little, (not a promising name one would have thought), Lee's Venus, Snook's Beauty, How's Cupid and Taylor's Ploughboy. The National Auricula Society was founded in 1872.

Jane Loudon describes the four main kinds clearly and simply in *Gardening For Ladies* – 'the green-edged, the Greyedged, the White-edged and the Selfs. When the stigma is seen above the anthers it is called pin-eyed, and is esteemed of very little value by the florists.'

For a while auriculas lapsed into undeserved obscurity, but once again they are coming back into our gardens, although many old favourites have disappeared forever.

Wallflower

Cheiranthus   Friendship in adversity

Defying time, the wallflower in its wild state still does sentry
duty on crumbling battlements and castle walls. Because it is
so often found growing on the ruined arches of old monasteries and forsaken halls, it is regarded as the emblem of
friendship in adversity, and no Gothic romance was once considered complete without the screech of owl, the flittering of
bats, and the wallflower.

Canon Vaughan wrote of the wallflowers of Winchester:
'Nothing can exceed the beauty of the Close walls when the
familiar gillyflower gilds with its pale yellow blossoms the grey
masonry. . . . It covers the broken walls, and the picturesque
ruins of Wolvesey hard by, in glorious profusion.'[1]

During the French Revolution, the Parisian rabble dragged
down and shattered all the royal monuments in Saint Denis.
Some time later, the poet Treneuil visited the heaps of sculptured fragments lying in an obscure corner of the abbey. They
were covered with fragrant wallflowers.

But although it shows a fondness for the ecclesiastical and
the upper class in architecture, no one could accuse the wallflower of snobbery, for where would the cottage garden be
without it?

> The single blood-walls, of a luscious smell,
> Old fashioned flowers which housewives love so well —[2]

grew, and still grow, beside old brick paths and on narrow
window-ledges, and on garden walls where they were affection-
ately known as Bloody Warriors. They are 'very delightful to
be set under a Parlour or lower Chamber Window,' wrote
Francis Bacon in his essay 'On Gardens', and more than four
hundred years later, who would disagree?

82

PLATE I

Wild Flowers

Lithograph by J. M. Kronheim, from *The Christian Garland*, c. 1880.

PLATE II

Lily of the Valley and Anemone

Hand-coloured engraving, after the original drawing by
Louisa Anne Twamley. From *The Romance of Nature*,
Louisa Anne Twamley, 1836.

In cottage gardens they are still valued as bee-flowers, and indeed Bee-flowers they are sometimes called, and they were often planted near apple trees to encourage the fruiting. 'The Husbandman preserveth it most in his Bee-Garden, for it is wondrous sweet and affordeth much honey.'[3]

Its early and loveliest name of Chevisaunce means 'comfort', and it was also known as Winter or March Gilliflower; and Cheiry, a shortened form of Cheiranthus, the name given to it by Linnaeus. The yellow single wallflowers from which the deeper colours were later developed were known to the ancient Greeks. They came to us in the Middle Ages from Southern and Central Europe. In Palestine the deep-coloured flowers were called the 'blood-drops of Christ'.

Wallflowers were worn by the troubadours and minstrels, and they are many times mentioned in the old Provençal ballads. There is a Scottish legend, retold by Herrick, in which a maiden, flying to her lover, falls from a wall and dies.

> Love, in pitty of the deed,
> And her loving-lucklesse speed,
> Turn'd her to this Plant, we call
> Now, the Flower of the Wall.[4]

Gerard recommends 'the oyle of Wallflowers' as 'good to be used to annoint a paralyticke'.

To Dion Clayton Calthrop they were gipsy-like, with a scent of the wind on the road, but to me they speak of still days and hot stone.

Those of us with never an abbey, a castle, nor even a ruined wall, must sow our wallflowers from a packet, and for us V. Sackville-West describes the wallflower nursery bed.

> Therefore the while, your current wallflowers blow,
> Bronze as a pheasant, ruby as old wine
> Held up against the light, – in string-straight line
> Next year's supply on seed-bed you shall sow.[5]

Daisy

Gentleness and innocence

There is a freshly-laundered look about the daisy, even a hint
of starch in the early morning petals. It is a dapper little thing.

> Say earth, why hast thou got thee new attire,
> And stick'st thy habit full of daisies red?[1]

I think everyone loves it except proud owners of perfect lawns.
Although banished from most good tennis lawns, Sir Herbert
Maxwell noticed in the gardens of Culzean in Ayrshire, that
where the lines of the court had been marked with whitewash,
the grass had died, and had subsequently been replaced with
dark lines of daisy leaves. These, of course, were kept mown
with the grass; but how much pleasanter it would have been
to have a court marked out with daisies than with whitewash.

It is all things to all men. To W. H. Davies it spoke, I do
not know why, of 'the cold dark grave'. It is odd that such a
cheerful looking flower should speak of graves, but Walter
Savage Landor's verse,

> Quieter is his breath, his breast more cold
> Than daisies in the mould,

has a chilling sound, and, after all, we do speak of pushing up
the daisies when we talk of death. But to John Davidson
'Glow-worm-like the daisies peer', which is poetic but in-
accurate, for at glow-worm time, when darkness falls, the
daisies, far from glimmering, disappear into the night, as John
Clare knew when he wrote of watching daisies 'button into
buds'.

To Wordsworth, the daisy was 'a nun demure, of lowly
port;' 'a starveling in a scanty vest,' and 'a little Cyclops with
one eye, Staring to threaten and defy,' and in Beaumont and

Fletcher's *Two Noble Kinsmen*, daisies are 'smell-less, but most quaint'. Chaucer rose early to see it.

> In my bed, there dawneth me no day,
> That I n'am up and walking in the mead,
> To see this flow'r against the sunne spread,

and in the evening he went to see

> – how it will go to rest,
> For feare of night, so hateth it the darknesse.[2]

To Burns it is the 'wee, modest, crimson-tipped flower', but to Andrew Young, 'an impudent juggler who spreads his mat in a crowded street, it spreads its leaf-rosette on the ground and, standing on it, defies interference from other plants.'[3]

W. H. Hudson writes of 'cycling over the high down country near Dorchester. I caught sight of what looked to me like a broad band of snow lying across the green hills. Coming to it I found the old Roman road, which is there very distinct and has a closer turf and a brighter green than the downs it lies across, so thickly overgrown with daisies that the crowded flowers were actually touching and had obliterated the green colour of the ground under them. It was a wonderful sight, for all these millions of small blossoms occupied the road only, not a daisy being seen on the green down on either side, and the loveliness was of so rare a quality, so rich yet so delicate, a beauty almost supernatural, that I could not bear to walk or ride on it. It was like a road leading to some unearthly brighter place – some paradise of flowers.'[4]

And yet the folding up at evening of each minute flower star in that milky way, would change the landscape in a few minutes from white to green, and from green to grey. One is reminded by this description of Elizabeth Barrett Browning's

> And open pastures where you scarcely tell
> White daisies from white dew.

In spite of its reputation for innocence, Parkinson says that 'Some would have the name Bellis to be taken from Belus the

king of Danaus, whose fifty daughters, being married to their
fifty husbands, did the first night of their marriage make a
mournful massacre, every one of their husbands except one;'
though what this bit of butchery had to do with the innocent
daisy is not clear. The story must soon have been forgotten,
because the roots of daisies were frequently boiled in milk and
given to little puppies to keep them small, which was why it was
known as the dog daisy, so it is said. The most likely explana-
tion of the name, however, is that, like the dog rose and the
dog violet, the dog daisy is a common flower. It seems that not
only puppies were fed with daisy roots to keep them small.
The story of the fairy Milkah tells how she fed her royal
foster-child on the berries of dwarf elder, and on daisy roots
to keep him tiny; a superstition that arose from the notion that
everything had the property of bestowing its own characteristics on others.

> She robbed dwarf-elder of their fragrant fruit,
> And fed him early with the daisy root,
> Whence through his veins the powerful juices ran,
> And formed the beauteous miniature of man.[5]

Everyone knows that it is a sign of spring when you can
stand on nine daisies with one foot; and that lambs lie down to
sleep when the daisies close. The Welsh call it Trembling
Star, though it seems too toughened by life's vicissitudes, by
grazing animals and hikers' boots, and the close-set blades of
mowers, to tremble overmuch.

In France it is called Paquerette, because it blossoms most
at Easter, and country girls played the 'He loves me, he loves
me not,' game as they pulled off the petals one by one; just as it
was played in English meadows.

> 'La blanche et simple Paquerette,
> Que ton coeur consulte surtout
> Dit: ton amant, tendre fillette,
> T'aime, un peu, beaucoup, point du tout.'

Even the roots were of comfort to the lovelorn. 'They who wish to have pleasant dreams of the loved and absent, should put daizy roots under their pillow.'[6]

In the northern counties of England it was called Bairns-wort, the child's flower, and sometimes Bruisewort, because it was mentioned in old herbals as a remedy for bruises. Its ancient name of Herb Margaret had almost disappeared by the middle of the nineteenth century.

But when this 'bright flower, whose home is everywhere,'[7] was brought into cultivation it grew larger and more double, and with greater variation of colour. Double daisies are flowers not to be overlooked, for they are cheerful and compact, with a long blooming season, but keep them from beds which border your lawns, or you will find them hob-nobbing happily with their poorer relatives and abusing your hospitality.

Walter de la Mare in *Come Hither* says: 'Pliny, after describing its "five and fifty little leaves, set round about it in the manner of fine pales", thought the daisy was useless. "These be flowers of the meadows, and most of such are of no use at all."

'No use at all, none,' agreed Walter de la Mare, 'Except only to make a skylark of every heart whose owner has eyes in his head for a daisy's simple looks, its marvellous making, and the sheer happiness of their multitudes wide open in the sun or round-headed and adrowse in the evening twilight.'

Anemone

These good-natured painted ladies of the garden ask for little care and attention. Plant them point upwards at intervals throughout the year, and they will reward you at similar intervals with medallions of rich colour; cardinal red, purple, violet, shocking pink and white. Bring them into the house, drop them into a pewter mug, and there, making game of the dedicated flower arranger, they will glow their psychedelic hearts out for three weeks or more, asking only to be topped up when the water level sinks.

This method of planting at intervals has been practised for more than three hundred years, for it is mentioned in the advice given by John Parkinson to the lady gardener. 'Many of them [anemones] will beare flowers the second yeare, if the place where you sow them, be not annoyed with the smoake of Brewers, Dyers, or Maultkils, which if it be, then will they never thrive well . . . I cannot [gentlewomen] withold one other secret from you, which is to informe you how you may so order Anemones, that after all others ordinarily are past, you may have them in flower for two or three moneths longer than are to be seene with any other, that useth not this course I direct you . . . if you will keepe some roots out of the ground unplanted, untill February, March, and Aprill, and plant some at one time, and some at another, you shall have them beare flower according to their planting.'

The single red anemone, the flower of Holy Week, grew at the foot of the Cross on Calvary, and was believed to have been turned from white to red by the blood of Christ. It abounds in Palestine, and it is thought by some to have been the original of the 'lilies of the field' of the Bible. In spite of the brilliance of its colour, it is a flower of sadness and death; the death of

Adonis and the death of Christ. It was dedicated to the Virgin, and called Our Lady's Petticoats.

D. H. Lawrence writes of the scarlet anemones growing wild in Tuscany, 'one of the loveliest scarlet apparitions in the world. The inner surface of the Adonis-blood is as fine as velvet, – and yet there is no suggestion of pile, not so much as on a velvet rose. And from this inner smoothness issues the red colour, perfectly pure and unknown of earth, no earthiness, and yet solid, not transparent – It is just pure condensed red, of a velvetiness without velvet, and a scarlet without glow.'[1]

'The double bloody lily,' they were sometimes called, 'but the colour is not well expressed by that term: it is a deep Scarlet but not Blood-colour.'[2] Edward FitzGerald wrote of their bold appearance, 'eyeing the sun manfully'.[3]

The violet-coloured anemone, so splendid a foil for the scarlet, was also described by Lawrence, growing in its wild state in Tuscany. 'They are curious, these great, dark violet anemones. You may pass them on a grey day, or at evening or early morning, and never see them. But as you come along in the full sunshine, they seem to be baying at you with all their throats, baying deep purple into the air. Whereas when they are shut, they have a silkiness and a curved head, like the curve of an umbrella handle and a peculiar outward colourlessness that makes them quite invisible.'[1]

The flowers were once considered to have magical properties, and the old herbalists recommended that everyone should gather the first anemone he saw, repeating at the same time, 'I gather thee for a remedy against disease.'[4] It was then placed in a scarlet cloth and kept until the gatherer became ill, when it was tied round the neck, or arm of the patient.

'Many newe and strange kindes' were brought back by travellers during the reign of Elizabeth I. Gerard had twelve different sorts in his garden in 1597, and Parkinson said of these 'pleasant and delightsome' flowers that 'the sight of them doth enforce an earnest longing desire in the minde of any one to be a possessor of some of them at least'. At that time it had not been given its Greek name of anemone, but was commonly called Rose Parsley. Turner, the herbalist, said that 'it maye be called in English Rose Persely, because there groweth a floure like a single rose in ye middle of this herbe, which is very lyke persely in the leaves which are about the rose'.[5]

They were first grown commercially for the cut-flower trade in Victoria's days, and we still welcome these pleasant and delightsome flowers when the first bunches arrive from Cornwall and the Scillies early in the year.

Violet

Viola   Modesty

We seem to have been misinformed about the violet.

'The violet is not modest! Why did you say that the violet was modest? because it conceals itself under the grass? The violet does not conceal itself under the grass, it is concealed there by nature. No one is modest from being born in an humble and obscure situation – the violet is born in the grass, it is true; but what stratagems does it employ to get out of it! Besides the colours which it affects, and which make it easily distinguished, does it not exhale that delicious perfume which would reveal it even to a blind man? The modest violet, indeed! do you see to what it has attained? It has covered the heads of the Church, the bishops and the arch-bishops, with its livery; black is the mourning of all the world, violet has become the black of kings, and the mourning of the purple – the modest violet! But observe its allurements, its coquetries: here it is white, there it is as double as a little rose, white, violet, grey, and rose-coloured! . . . The violet modest! Go to the opera, two hundred women have bouquets of violets in their hands'.[1]

Alphonse Karr might have added that, thrust under the noses of top-hatted gentlemen by the flower girls of Piccadilly, they weren't so very modest either. There is a lot more about the immodest violet which I would enjoy quoting, in a charming little book, written in an age that is farther away than the Greeks and Romans. Try and beg, borrow or steal a copy of Karr's *A Tour Round My Garden*, translated into English by the Reverend J. G. Wood, and published by Routledge in the 1850s. You will probably only be able to acquire it by the latter method for it is scarce, but it is worth the risk.

Keats took the more conventional view. In a letter to J. H.

Reynolds, dated 1818, he wrote, 'How beautiful are the retired flowers! How would they lose their beauty were they to
throng into the highway, crying out, 'Admire me, I am a violet!
Dote upon me, I am a primrose!' Now violets grow on Keats'
grave in the burial ground at the foot of Mount Testaccio.
When in 1861 Severn, the friend who was with him when his
short life ended, returned to Rome after an absence of twenty
years, the custodian of the cemetery complained that he could
not keep the violets on the grave, for they were so constantly
picked in remembrance of the poet. But Severn only answered,
'Sow and plant twice as much!'[2]

'That which above all others, yields the sweetest Smell in
the Air, is the violet, especially the White double Violet,
which comes twice a year, about the middle of April, and about
Bartholomew-tide,' wrote Sir Francis Bacon; and Henry
Lyte, the herbalist, described them thus: 'There be two sorts of
violets, the garden and the wylde violet. The garden violets
are of a fayre, darke, or shining deepe blewe colour, and a very
pleasant and amiable smelle. The wylde violets are without
savour, and of a fainte blewe or pale colour.'[3]

Cultivated violets have served many purposes for many
people. So highly regarded was the sweet violet, *V. odorata*,
that it was made the symbol of Athens, and both Greeks and
Romans wore it in wreaths and chaplets. It was used as a cure
for wounds; bound round the head for headaches; taken as
a sedative, and made into wine. The young leaves were
fried and eaten with sugar and lemon juice; the flowers
were sprinkled on salads, and in the reigns of Charles I and
Charles II a violet conserve was made and enjoyed.

In France the violet was the secret emblem of the followers
of Napoleon. During his absence they wore violet-coloured
watch ribbons, and violet rings with the device, 'I will appear
again in the spring,' and he was toasted by the name of
'Corporal Violet'. It had been Josephine's favourite flower,
always given to her by Napoleon on their wedding anniversary.
Before leaving for St Helena he took a bunch of violets to her
tomb, and he was welcomed back after his escape from Elba on

20 March 1815, with violets. When he was dead, he was found to be wearing a medallion containing a lock of Josephine's hair, and some dried violets.

One could go on and on with similar romantic tales – how it was loved by the Empress Eugenie; how every night for thirty years the actress, Madame Clairon, drank an infusion of violets given her each morning by an admirer. Tyler Whittle mentions, among the conceits and follies of eccentric gardeners, 'the garden of the French romantic which was entirely given over to the cultivation of Violets, so that he could present his mistress with a fresh bunch of Violets every single day for thirty years.'[4] He names no names, but surely there cannot have been two ageing mistresses, even in the whole of France, receiving daily bunches of violets over so long a period? No wonder Madame Clairon was driven to the making of violet tisanes every evening as a means of disposing as politely as possible of so embarrassing an offering.

The violet has given so much pleasure to so many people that it might be forgiven if it did grow a little immodest over the years. Take Charles Lamb's grandmother, for instance: 'I do not know which pleased grandma best, when we carried her home a lapful of eggs, or a few violets; for she was particularly fond of violets.'[5]

Fanny Kemble, when her disastrous marriage to Pierce Butler in Philadelphia was still new, found that her love of flowers met stiff opposition from the gardener, whose only interest was in vegetables. When she reproached him for not pointing out to her the early violets blooming along a sunny walk, he replied, 'Well, Ma'am, I quite forgot them violets. You see them flowers are such frivolous creatures.'[6]

William Cobett had a pleasant encounter at Godstone: 'At and near Godstone the gardens are all very neat; and, at the inn, there is a nice garden well stocked with beautiful flowers in the season. I here saw, last summer, some double violets as large as small pinks, and the lady of the house was kind enough to give me some of the roots.'[7]

The violet is the traditional flower of Mothering Sunday,

the fourth Sunday in Lent, when small bunches are brought home in hot sticky hands from Sunday school.

There was an extraordinary story of an experiment in which potted violets were sent up in a balloon which was made stationary for a few days, after which 'these violets grew thrice the size of any that had ever bloomed in this firm set earth'.[8]

No wonder that this 'happy lowlie down', as it was called in Shakespeare's day, is a poet's flower.

> No rose but fades, no glory but must pass:
> No hue but dims: no precious silk but frets.
> Her beauty must go underneath the grass,
> Under the long roots of the violets.[9]

Forgive this note of sadness, but I simply cannot leave out poor Prewdence Baldwin, for Herrick's verse is her one claim to fame.

> In this little urn is laid
> Prewdence Baldwin, once my maid:
> From whose happy spark here let
> Spring the purple violet.[10]

Pansy

Like tabby cats and tortoise-shells, one could almost believe that these velvet-faced comedians go roaming the roof-tops at night, returning to their beds before the milkman calls, with that comic-innocent look on their faces.

Is it the pansy's funny face that has earned it more pet names than almost any other flower? Johnny-jump-up, Three-faces-in-a-hood, Ladies' Delight, Flamy (because its colours may be seen in the flame of a wood fire), and Heartsease?

> Heartsease, like a gallant bold,
> In his cloth of silver and gold.[1]

In Scotland it was known as a Stepmother; so called because of the large lower petal with a 'daughter' on either side, and two upper petals which are the stepdaughters. In Germany there is a variation of this; for the stepmother sits on two stools, which are the points of the calyx, one point for each true daughter; but there is only one point or stool for the two step-daughters to sit on.

In many ancient herbals it was called *Herba trinitas*, and dedicated to the Trinity because of its three colours – 'So God is three distinct persones; in one undivided Trinity, United in one eternal glory and divine majesty.'[2] Culpeper felt strongly on this subject. 'This is the herb,' he wrote 'which such physicians as are licensed to blaspheme by authority, without danger of having their tongues burned through with a hot iron, called an herb of Trinity.' He noted, however, that it is an excellent cure for the French pox. It was also considered handy to have about the house as a remedy for asthma and epilepsy, inflammation of the lungs and chest, and also for skin diseases in babies; but later it was less highly regarded, and

95

nearly, if not altogether, neglected, 'for fashion creeps even into our pill boxes'.[3]

There are two British wild species, *V. tricolor*, or three-coloured pansy, and *V. lutea*, the yellow mountain pansy. An article by Mr Thomson of Iver, in *The Floricultural Cabinet* of 1841, describes how the first garden pansies were cultivated. 'About seven or eight and twenty years ago, Lord Gambier brought me a few roots of the common yellow and white Heartsease, which he had gathered in the grounds at Iver, and requested that I would cultivate them. Always eager to please my worthy and ever-to-be-lamented master, I did so, saved the seed, and found that they improved beyond my most sanguine expectation. In consequence thereof I collected all the varieties that could be obtained. From Brown, of Slough, I had the blue; and from some other person, whose name I do not now recollect, a darker sort, said then to have been imported from Russia. These additions wonderfully improved my breeders. But still, though the varieties I soon obtained were multitudinous, their size was almost as diminutive as the originals. Nevertheless his lordship was pleased, and thus I was amply rewarded . . . I then began to think that some of my sorts were worthy of propagation; and this circumstance led me to give one, which took his lordship's fancy, a name. This was entitled Lady Gambier . . . Lady Gambier was the beauty of her tribe. . . . It was, indeed, in shape little more symmetrical than a child's windmill, but looked in size among the sisterhood like a giant surrounded by dwarfs. But the giant of those days would be a pigmy now, as Lady Gambier herself appeared in comparison with another flower, which I soon after raised, and which, on account of what I then considered its monstrous proportions, I christened Ajax. This I then thought could never be surpassed, and yet in shape it was as lengthy as a horse's head.'

From these, Show Pansies were developed, which gave place to the Fancy Pansies, first known as the Belgian Pansies, about 1848. From 1860 onwards Scotland became the source of the best cultivated pansies. 'Pansies like a climate that is sometimes "blae and bleuk", and England never sees that perfection of velvet pile on their purple faces that Scotland knows so well.'[4]

They were the favourite flowers of Mrs Siddons, the tragic actress, who grew them in her garden in Harrow Road. So great was her demand for purple pansies to fill her spring borders that her maid, who was sent out to obtain them, became known among the gardeners as 'Miss Heartsease'.

No summer garden is complete without its pansy border, but the odd pansy face which surprises us in winter is worth them all. 'The wind is icy, and the snow patches are still here, but in the nearest garden I can get to I saw — one yellow pansy staring up at the sun astonished and reproachful because it had bits of frozen mud stuck to its little cheeks.'[5]

And so, 'God send thee hartes ease. For it is mutch better with poverty to have the same, than to be a kynge, with a miserable mynde'.[2]

Forget-me-not

Myosotis   Forget me not

The gold-eyed forget-me-not, once the picture-postcard beauty of our grandmothers, has grown a little passé with the years. During two reigns it was woven in ribbons, embroidered on cushion-covers, embossed on valentines, painted on china, lithographed on scraps and ornamental texts, and painstakingly reproduced by young ladies in albums, accompanied by a few appropriate lines. It headed notepaper and menus, and was top favourite on birthday cards; and its pink and blue, cunningly reproduced in velvet, adorned many a fetching bonnet.

Perhaps the German legend of the knight who plunged into a river in order to pluck a bunch of the flowers for his lady-love, and failing to reach the bank, drowned before her very eyes, crying 'Forget me not,' as he sank, may have something to do with its waning popularity in this earth-bound age. Did the knight plunge in in full armour? Or was he just a poor swimmer? Or perhaps it was trying to say 'Vergiss mein nicht' in mid-stream that caused the catastrophe? At all events, the sooner he is forgotten, the better, one feels.

It was said that a garden of forget-me-nots sprang up on the field of Waterloo, in the following spring, in remembrance of the men who fell on both sides; an earlier version of the poppy fields of Flanders.

Myosotis means mouse-ear, in reference to the shape of its leaves. All the species were often called scorpion grass, from the curled flower heads which were thought to resemble a scorpion's tail, and were therefore expected to cure a scorpion's sting. 'The floures grow at the top of tender, flat, greene stalkes, blew of colour, and sometimes with a spot of

PLATE III

Auricula

Hand-coloured engraving from *Lectures on Botany*,
William Curtis, 1802. (Found in a botanical scrapbook.)

PLATE IV

Pansies

Hand-coloured engraving, after the original drawing by
Louisa Anne Twamley. From *The Romance of Nature*,
Louisa Anne Twamley, 1836.

yellow among the blew: the whole branch of floures do turne themselves likewise round like a scorpion's taile.'[1]

Forget-me-nots in bunches or in pots were sold in the Paris markets in the nineteenth century. They were also used by the Germans at this time to plant round their graves. A blue mist of forget-me-nots may be conventional, but it is still the best background to a tulip bed. From a distance it seems as though the bright flower-heads float like boats on regatta day, waiting for the starting pistol.

Francis Kilvert wrote in his diary of finding a silk book-marker with Forget-Me-Not embroidered on it. 'It was a gift from a child sweetheart. But from which? I gazed at the words conscience-stricken. Forget-Me-Not. And I had forgotten.'

Can it be that in order to remember we must first forget?

Lily of the Valley

Convallaria   Happiness and unconscious sweetness

The mini-skirted lilies of the valley arrive in May, and vanish
before the month has ended. All that underground work for
such a brief appearance; like a well-trained corps-de-ballet
they delight us and are gone. The twin green leaves retire
modestly into the background; a scarlet berry appears here
and there, but makes no great effort to attract our attention.

A native of Great Britain, these wild flowers were planted in
gardens by the middle of the sixteenth century. There are five
species, and among them, double, purple, pink and even
striped varieties could once be found. They were known by
country folk under many different names; May Lily, Our
Lady's Tears or Mary's Tears, because it grew from the tears
the Virgin shed at the foot of the Cross; Mugget, from the
French Muguet: and all sorts of variations of their botanical
name *Convallaria*, Lily Convalle or Conval Lily, Lilly Con-
stancy, and even nicer, Liriconfancie. Another Medieval name,
probably given by the monks, was Ladder-to-heaven, from
the step-like placing of the flowers on the stem.

The flowers were used to decorate churches, and when Lady
chapels were built in honour of the Virgin, lilies were placed
there whenever possible.

Long ago the lily of the valley was common on Hampstead
Heath, and also in St Leonard's Forest in Sussex. A local
legend explained its presence here as having sprung from the
blood shed by St Leonard, the patron saint of the district, in his
battle with a great and terrible dragon; and, as the botanist
Edward Hume says, 'anyone who, in this sceptical age, has
doubts, can go and see the flowers for himself.'[1]

In some small towns in Germany a bunch of lilies of the
valley was paid as rent, a token claimed originally for religious

purposes. They grew so freely in the woods of Hanover that it became the custom to make special expeditions to pick them on Whit Monday. 'Cottages are erected for the sale of coffee and other refreshments, and neither the pleasures of tobacco nor the twirling waltz are omitted on that occasion.'[2]

Lily picking excursions on a more modest scale, called lily-pics, used to be held in Sowley Wood, part of the ancient forest of Selwood, and Mrs Gaskell writes in *Wives and Daughters* of plans for a similar picnic, when the match-making Mrs Gibson says, 'Speaking of lilies of the valley, is it true that they grow wild in Hurstwood? It is not the season for them to be in flower yet; but when it is, I think we must take a walk there – with our luncheon in a basket – a little picnic, in fact . . . we could have a long day in the woods, and all come home to dinner – dinner with a basket of lilies in the middle of the table!'

In the West Country there were varying superstitions regarding the planting of lilies of the valley. In Devonshire it was considered unlucky to plant a bed of them, as the plant would probably die within twelve months. In other parts it was believed to be unlucky to transplant them. Unlucky it may be, but tedious it certainly is, to disentangle and replant those snaky white roots, and the whole idea was probably thought up by some unenthusiastic, underpaid gardener. The roots were used in medicine, and the leaves, prepared with lime, yielded a dye useful to manufacturers.

Although it had its moments of gaiety when it took part in lily-pics and the Helston Furry dance, it is at heart a quiet, unassuming plant, and best described by Alphonse Karr as a 'perfumed pearl'. She

> – silent and alone puts on her suit,
> And sheds her lasting perfume, but for which
> We had not known there was a thing so sweet
> Hid in the gloomy shade.[3]

Crown Imperial

Fritillaria   Majesty and Power

John Parkinson, who in 1629 dedicated his best of all garden books to Henrietta Maria, Queen of Charles I – 'Accept, I beseech your Majestie, this speaking Garden, that may informe you in all the particulars of your store, as well as wants, when you cannot see any of them fresh upon the ground,'[1] – chose the Crown Imperial for his opening chapter. Twenty years afterwards he saw his royal patroness deprived of her husband and the British crown with one stroke of an axe. No wonder that there are tears in each flower's down-turned cup.

'In the bottom of each of these bels there is placed six drops of most cleare shining sweet water, in taste like sugar, resembling in shew faire orient pearls; the which drops if you take away, there do immediately appeare the like: notwithstanding if they may be suffered to stand still in the flower according to his own nature, they will never fall away, no not if you strike the plant untill it be broken.'[1]

The bulb is of the lily family, but its origin is not clear. It seems to have been unknown to the ancients. 'The Crown Imperiall for his stately beautifulnesse deserveth the first place in this our Garden of Delight. . . . This plant was first brought from Constantinople into these Christian Countries, and by the relation of some that sent it, groweth naturally in the woods in Persia.'[1]

It was first known as the Persian Lily. Charles de l'Ecluse, otherwise known as Clusius, introduced it into Vienna in 1576. Twenty-one years later Gerard received some plants from Poland which he grew in his garden in Holborn. The bulbs were much sought after, and as costly as those of the tulip. It is still an expensive bulb, and whether its price, or its peculiar smell, a combination of onion and fox, is to blame or not, it is not common in modern gardens, but in the rich man's garden, as well as the cottage plot, the grand orange and yellow clumps, established over long periods of time, are an impressive sight. Those bulbs which have remained in suitable soil for two or three years may send up a stem which carries two or three whorls of flowers one above the other, which is called a triple crown. But from *In Veronica's Garden* comes a warning: 'they resent disturbance as much as an Irish tenant.'[2]

'In my youth they were rather sniffed at and called a cottage plant,' said that vigorous Edwardian writer of the *Potpourri* books, Mrs Earle, but she adds, 'I wonder if anyone who thought them vulgar ever took the trouble to pick off one of the down-hanging bells and turn it up to see the six drops of clear water in the six white cups with black rims?'[3]

An equally prolific garden writer of the same period, E.V.B., whose initials stand for the Honourable Mrs Evelyn Boyle, also wrote in their defence, 'I think we may well forgive our Crown Imperials this smell, however, for the stately show they make; and if taste and fashion did not change with flowers as with other things, they might still be among the choice favourites of spring.'[4]

> Then her gay gilded front th' Imperial Crown
> Erects aloft, and with a scornful Frown
> O'erlooks the subject Plants, while humbly they
> Wait round, and Homage to her Highness pay.[5]

In France, at one period, attempts were made to cultivate the bulbs, which contain starch, as a substitute for potatoes. The experiment failed, which is regrettable. Sausage and Crown Imperials would add an exotic charm to our luncheon menus.

Fritillary

Fritillaria   I can find no meaning for the fritillary,
                     The Language of Flowers is dumb.

Fritillaries always make me think of the Army and Navy
Stores. They have an air of quality and subdued refinement, like
elderly ladies in their summer voiles. But could this description fit the same flower as Vita Sackville-West's 'sinister
fritillary of malice'? 'The sinister fritillary Meleagris, with its
checkering of ashen rose and green and black, has no name
more suitable for its strange and sinister appearance than
Lazarus's Bell. Some village Baudelaire must have seen in it
the bell worn by lepers that warned men of their terrible
approach.'[1]

Gerard says that they were greatly esteemed 'for the
beautifying of our gardens and the bosoms of the beautiful'.
Since they were highly expensive, they presumably only beauti-
fied expensive bosoms, and as they were also known as Snake's
Head Fritillaries their connection with Cleopatra seems ob-
vious.

That they also had, and lost, other names, such as the
Lapwing Flower, and the Ginny Hen Flower, Frog Cup and
Fraw Cup, we can read in 'Sir' John Hill's *Eden: or, a Compleat
Body of Gardening*: 'This is an old inhabitant of our Gardens,
pleasing by its Particularity and for being raised with little
Trouble. . . . Our Gardener's Names of Chequer'd Lilly, and
Chequer'd Daffodill are wrong even for the vulgar.'

Another name, less vulgar and now forgotten, was, 'Narcissus Caparonius, of the name of the first finder thereof, called
Noel Caparon, an Apothecary, dwelling in Orleance, at the
time he first found it, and was shortly after the finding thereof
taken away in the Massacre in France.'[2] Whether Caparon
brought the fritillary bulb with him on his flight to England

after the Massacre of St Bartholomew on 24 August 1572, or whether he was killed and the bulb brought by some other refugee is not known. The name fritillary comes from 'Fritillus, which divers doe take for the Chesse borde or table whereon they play.'[2]

John Tradescant the elder, bought fritillaries from Cornelis Cornellison of Haarlem in 1611, but by the end of the eighteenth century they were found growing wild in England, probably a garden escape. It is now a rare wild flower that grows plentifully in the restricted areas in which it is to be found.

Just as the peony, the sunflower and the rose are painters' flowers, so the fritillary is a writers' flower. More has been said, and better, about the fritillary than about almost any other flower, since its bowed head and the grave quietness of its colouring imposes a restraint upon the too often unrestrained pen of the flower lover.

Geoffrey Grigson says that 'anyone living in the North or West, outside the fritillary counties, should walk at least once in a fritillary field before he dies'.[3] If that is not possible, he should read Andrew Young's *A Retrospect of Flowers*; John Vaughan's *The Music of Wild Flowers*; W. H. Hudson's *The Book of a Naturalist*, and the chapter 'Bloody Warriors, Weeping Widows,' in C. Henry Warren's pleasant book, *Content With What I Have*. I have not seen a fritillary field in bloom, and although I grow them in a small corner of my garden, I shall not be content until I do.

Iris

One of the earliest cultivated plants, the iris, the flower of
light, may be seen in bas-relief at Karnak. It was imported
into Egypt some 1400 years before the birth of Christ. It was
sculptured on the brow of the sphynx. The Greeks prized it
for its medicinal uses; Pliny gave elaborate instructions for the
ceremonial gathering of the roots.

The yellow water-iris, *I. pseudacorus*, has the most interesting history of all the irises, for it was the fleur-de-lys or fleur-
de-luce, the emblem of royalty of Clovis, the first King of
France. Its three large petals, symbolizing Faith, Wisdom and
Valour, were placed on the sceptres of the kings of France,
and at the time of the Crusades the flower was known as
Fleur-de-Louis. The number of fleur-de-lys in the arms of
France was reduced to three in the reign of Charles VI about
1381. The symbol was outlawed during the French Revolution in 1792, and hundreds of men and women found wearing
it were condemned to death. Reinstated with Louis XVIII in
1814, it was continued with Charles X, and again outlawed in
1830 when Charles was dethroned.

But England, too, used the flower as an emblem, for
Edward III added it to the arms of England. Shakespeare
mentions it in *Henry VI, Part I*, when a messenger says,
'Cropped are the flower-de-luces on your arms; Of England's
coat one half is cropped away'. It was not until 1800 that
George III replaced the fleur-de-lys with the shamrock.

In addition to its heraldic uses, it was employed on old
maps and charts to distinguish the north point. It was first
used on the mariner's compass by Flavio Gioia of Amalfi, in
honour of the King of Naples, who was a member of the

French royal family. Gioia also introduced the magnet into navigation.

The yellow iris gave a yellow dye from its flower and a black dye from its roots. The latter was used in the making of ink. The roots were also used to scent and starch laundry, and the powdered root, orris root, was mixed with ordinary hair powder and sold as violet powder for the hair. It was supposed to cure toothache, and so was made into 'corals' for teething babies. It was suspended in beer casks to prevent the beer becoming stale, and in wine casks to give bouquet. The common blue flower was mixed with alum by the monks to produce a green pigment for the illumination of manuscripts. All this and coffee too, for the roasted seeds were used instead of coffee; but the cautious Anne Pratt said, 'We cannot recommend them, for their wholesomeness is doubtful'.[1]

In the south of England it was called Levers, from laefer, a flag; and sometimes Flag-flower, Dagger-flower and Dragon-flower. In Scotland it might be Luggs, or Water Skegs, or Segg, a corruption of sedge, a small sword. Because of its sword-like leaves it is the Japanese emblem of a warrior.

However, it is the common flag of the cottage garden that is the Poorman's iris, with its heavy falls like velvet curtains, and its great range of colour, from white to deepest purple-black, 'a more brilliant prism than Noah saw in the clouds,' as old FitzGerald wrote in a letter to his friend Bernard Barton in 1844. He was very attached to his garden, and wrote about it in his letters to his many friends, whether they were interested or no. 'I remember you did not desire to hear about my garden which is now gorgeous with red poppies and lilac irises,' he wrote to Frederick Tennyson on 19 June 1849.

More than three hundred years ago, Thomas Hanmer wrote in his *Garden Book*, 'Of the Great Flagged Irises wee have severall colours, as deepe blew, pale blew, ash colour, white, purple, Flesh Colour, and some few with two or more colours, one of which hath blew standards and peach falls. Of the other Flaggs, that are not Dwarfes, there are the White, the Yellow, the light Blew, the Deeper Blew, the Purple, the

Chalcedonian, or blacke Grey, the pure white-edged and stript downe the backe with light watchet, [light blue], the Purple vein'd with Yellow, and many other varietys, too long to bee here mentioned.'

A flower so useful, so beautiful; content with almost any soil, except an over-rich one; and with half-shade, if sun is hard to spare: 'There is scarce a cottage garden round about in Aberdeenshire without its iris clumps. I know a little garden there, that grows them in a wonderful double line, milk-white. "Aye", responds the gude-wife when the great number of her white flowers is admired, "I just slice 'em like ing'ons (onions) and digs them in".'[2]

Here is a sight of irises in Tuscany: 'Then the lovely pale-lilac irises will come out in all their showering abundance of tender, proud, spiky bloom, till the air will gleam with mauve, and a new crystalline lightness will be everywhere. The iris is half-wild, half-cultivated. The peasants sometimes dig up the roots, iris root, orris root — So, in May, you will find ledges and terraces, fields just lit up with the mauve light of irises, and so much scent in the air, you do not notice it, you do not even know it. It is all the flowers of the iris, before the olive invisibly blooms.'[3]

And here is a sad little description, perfect as a miniature, of irises after a storm:

> Hailstones scarred
> The tender green, and battered hard
> Upon the irises, poor maids
> Who fell, and died on their own blades.[4]

Columbine

Strange that the columbine is the flower of two birds, the eagle and the dove; two birds so different. It is called columbine from its likeness to a cluster of doves, with beaks that meet in the centre and tails outspread, like the doves of Pliny's vase. It was given its Latin name, *Aquilegia*, because the inverted tubes at the base of the flower are like the curved claws of an eagle. To complicate matters still further, it was formerly called *Herba Leonis*, because it was thought to be the favourite plant of the lion. 'Columbine is called of the later Herbarists, Aquilegia: of some, Herba Leonis, or the herbe wherein the Lion doth delight.'[1]

Both single and double columbines grew in Gerard's day. 'They are used especially to decke the gardens of the curious, garlands and houses,' he says. 'The flowers hereof be very double, that is to say, many of those little flowers (having the form of birds) are thrust one into the belly of another, sometimes blew, often white, and otherwhiles of mixt colours, as nature list to plaie with hir little ones.'[1]

To the country children they were known as Granny Bonnets in England and Grannies Mutch in Scotland. It was also called Cocksfoot. The short spurred variety grew wild in Great Britain, but only in certain places. Walter de la Mare writes of them growing on the Downs,

> This air breathed milky sweet
> With nodding columbine –

and W. H. Hudson found a rare pleasure in discovering them in a Wiltshire village. 'It was in Wiltshire that I found my first columbines, in a vast thicket of furze, may, and black-thorn covering about twenty acres of ground. The plants were

tall, the thin wiry stems being two or three feet long, and produced few leaves, but flowers as large as those of the garden
plant. An old keeper who had charge of the ground, told me
he had known the flower from his boyhood, and that formerly
he could fill a barrow with "collarbinds", as he called them,
any day. It was a rare pleasure to see that columbine in its own
home — the big blue quaint flower that looked at you from its
shelter of rough furze and thorn bushes; and for the first time
in my life I admired it since in the garden, where as a rule its
peculiar beauty is dimmed by other garden blooms, it has an
inharmonious setting. . . . This great find made me think that
I had come into a columbine country, and I set out to look for
it, but failed to find or even hear of it anywhere in that district
except at one spot on the border of Wilts and Dorset. This was
a tiny rustic village hidden away among high downs, one of the
smallest, loveliest, most out-of-the-world villages in England.
. . . So rare was it for a stranger to appear in this lost village
that half the population, all the forty schoolchildren included,
were eager to talk to me all the time I spent in it, and they all
knew all about the columbine. It had been abundant about
half a mile from the village by the hedges and among the furze
bushes, and every summer the children were accustomed to go
out and gather the flowers, and they were seen in every
cottage; and as a result of this misuse the flower had been
extirpated.'[2]

John Clare speaks of the columbine as a wild flower that has
been introduced to the cottage garden:

> The columbines, stone blue, or deep night brown,
> Their honeycomb-like blossoms hanging down.
> Each cottage garden's fond adopted child,
> Though heaths still claim them where they yet grow wild.[3]

The adopted child, *A. canadensis*, which grew in John
Tradescant's garden was introduced into England in 1640,
and it is from these that the lovely long-spurred varieties of
today have been developed. Now they can be grown in varying heights, from miniature rock plants to long-spurred giants,

but the dragonfly hybrids, which come in pink, crimson, blue, yellow and white, and do not exceed about eighteen inches in height, are best for the front of the border.

Chaucer mentions it as one of the eight plants which served as remedies against the plague. It was later thought to be 'effectuall to women in travell of childe, to procure a speedie deliverie'.[4]

On the whole, it might be advisable to avoid the long spurred variety.

Honeysuckle

Lonicera   Rustic beauty and affection

I was not a country child, and I had probably never seen the
flower, when I used to sit under the keys of our piano with my
head against the sounding-board in order to experience the
full resonance, listening to my grandmother singing inno-
cently to her own accompaniment, 'You are my honey –
honeysuckle, I am your bee.' When eventually I did see it,
with its twining stem and creamy, heavy-scented cornucopia,
it was everything I felt a flower ought to be.

The name Lonicera was given to it by Linnaeus in honour of
Adam Lonicer, a German botanist who died in 1586. It was
called by country people Woodbine or Woodbind, from its
twining habit; Ladies' Fingers, Suckling, and sometimes
Caprifoly, meaning goat-leaf, from a belief that the leaves were
the favourite food of goats. There are three British species,
and it is one of our early climbers, having been known since
the eighth century. Gerard mentions a double variety which
'groweth now in my Garden, and many others likewise in
great plenty, although not long since, very rare and hard to be
found, except in the garden of some diligent Herbarists.'

Different species of honeysuckle are to be found in Switzerland, Italy, North America, Russia and China, and it is a
much loved flower in Japan. It is a bee plant, and in an old
herbal it says, 'If the beehives be anoynted with the jus of hir
leeves, the been schalt not goo away: the housbondes kept his
swarmes in tyme of yere by such anoyntynge'.[1]

Cottagers used to apply the juice of the leaves as a cure for
bee-stings, and for a mouth wash, which caused the learned
Dr Culpeper to remark somewhat sharply, 'It is a plant so
common, that everyone that hath eyes knows it, and he that
hath none, cannot read a description, if I should write it. . . .
Dr. Tradition, that grand introducer of errors, that hater of

truth, lover of folly, and the mortal foe to Dr. Reason, hath taught the common people to use the leaves or flowers of this plant in mouth-water, and by long continuance of time, hath so grounded it in the brains of the vulgar, that you cannot beat it out with a beetle . . . then judge if old Dr. Tradition (who may well be honoured for his age, but not for his goodness) hath not so poisoned the world with errors before I was born, that it was never well in its wits since, and there is great fear it will die mad.'

Although it may be allowed, like a poor relation, some inconspicuous corner in the gardens of the wealthy, it remains the flower of the cottage garden and the country lane where 'the Honisuckle that groweth wilde in every hedge although it be very sweete yet doe I not bring into my garden, but let it rest in his owne place to serve their senses that travell by it, or have no garden.'[2]

Its tough stems, that follow the sun from east to west in their windings, were used by country people to bind brooms. Prefacing the scene where Prue Sarn of *Precious Bane* watched the magical emergence of the dragonflies, she says, 'I went down by the mere to gather honeysuckle wrathes to bind besoms,' and in this pleasant rural scene they are put to another use: 'Down the lane come two hard-worked farm-horses, their heads wreathed in honeysuckle to keep off the maddening flies'.[3]

Dorothy Wordsworth, who grew it in the cottage garden in Dovedale where she kept house for William, wrote in her diary on 3 June 1802, 'There are, I do believe, a thousand buds on the honeysuckle tree, all small and far from blowing, save one that is retired behind the twigs close to the wall, and as snug as a bird's nest.'

Walter Savage Landor loved it too. 'How sweetly smells the Honeysuckle In the hush'd night, as if the world were one Of utter peace and love and gentleness!'[4]

In the New Forest, the honeysuckle still plays host to the rare White Admiral, and there, like a good foster-mother, it sees it through its cycle of caterpillar, chrysalis and butterfly.

Peony

Paeonia   Bashful shame

To be painted by Manet, Monet, Renoir and Augustus John, not to mention the seventeenth century Dutch flower painters, and the many Chinese artists who loved it, is no small compliment, even for a flower. The peony seems to know that it is an artists' flower. It curves and lolls from its painted vase like some plump nude on a studio couch. Light reflects from its generous petals, which drop at last, like a pool of blood, or a drift of snow, on earth or table beneath.

It is one of the oldest of all the garden flowers, called after Paeon, the physician to the gods, and its Latin name *P. officinalis* is indicative of its connection with the apothecaries' garden. They were first mentioned by William Turner, when he published *The Names of Herbes in Greek, Latin, English, Dutch and French, with the common names that Herbaries and Apothecaries Use*. Paeon, a famous physician himself, and a pupil of Aesculapius, received the roots of the Paeony from the mother of Apollo on Mount Olympus.

Belonging to the buttercup family, it is a plant of many ancient beliefs and superstitions. The seeds were gathered in the waning moon and hung about the necks of children as a protection against the evil eye; and up to the end of the last century, beads were turned from the root, called 'piney beads', which were worn by small children to help them in cutting their teeth. The flowers were called 'peeny-roses', and an odd number of blooms in all the peony plants in your garden in one summer, signified a death in the family before the year was up.

The plant was used by our Saxon ancestors for flavouring purposes, and in Mongolia the seeds were used instead of tea.

The kernels were eaten as a condiment and the roots made into broth. I have peony roots and to spare in my garden, but I have little desire to try peony root broth. There is a pleasanter sounding recipe given by the herbalist Coles: 'Pounded with periwinkle leaves and strained with black cherry water and a good draught thereof taken three mornings fasting, the Peony restoreth lost wits, comforteth the senses and recovereth the speech.'[1] It has the added cachet that it was 'approved by the Lady Gage.'

The single peony appears to have been the earliest known, and it is native to many parts of Europe. The wild peony is known as the male peony, and the garden peony is the female.

'Physicians say, Male Peony roots are best; but Dr. Reason told me Male Peony was best for men, and Female Peony for Women; and he desires to be judged by his brother Dr. Experience.'

'Of the Male there is but one kind, but of the Females many, some bearing double, others single Flowers, resembling in shape the common red Rose; and these being usual I need not Elaborate to describe their kinds being mostly used for adorning Windows in House-Flower-pots.'[2]

There were at least eight varieties grown in the herb gardens of London, and they were said to cure no less than twenty diseases. The male flower was formerly to be found wild in the Cotswolds; in Betsome in the parish of Southfleet in Kent; and it still grows on Steep Holme, an island in the Bristol Channel. It is probably an escape from an ancient monastery garden, where it would have been grown for medicinal purposes.

The old double white was introduced to this country in the sixteenth century, for Gerard says, 'we do expect it from the lowe countries of Flaunders'.

There was a pleasant ceremony in the Gloucestershire village of Filkins, which was held on each Whit Tuesday until the First World War. The local Friendly Society marched through the village, its stewards carrying staves decorated with bunches of red peonies, but what particular association the flower had with the village, or with its Friendly Society, is now forgotten.

I have said no word of the beautiful tree peonies, in spite of their ancient history, for they were known as the Rich Man's flower, and were not introduced to Kew Gardens until 1787, when they remained too great a rarity for our Poorman's Nosegay.

Lilac

Lilacs seem to need companionship as much as robins do. The closer to the house they can get, the better they like it. Kipling calls them Doorway Lilacs, and Mary Webb describes a cottage that 'had sunk almost out of recognition in the foam of spring. Ancient lilacs stood about it and nodded purple-coroneted heads across its one chimney. Their scent bore down all other scents like a strong personality, and there was no choice but to think the thoughts of the lilac.'[1]

'Elizabeth', in whose German garden lilacs grew abund-antly, loved their scent. 'Oh, those lilac bushes! They are all out today, and the garden is drenched with the scent. I have brought in armfuls, the picking is such a delight, and every pot and bowl and tub in the house is filled with purple glory, and the servants think there is going to be a party and are extra nimble, and I go from room to room gazing at the sweetness, and the windows are all flung open so as to join the scent within to the scent without; and the servants gradually discover that there is no party, and wonder why the house should be filled with flowers for one woman by herself.'[2]

Did Elizabeth and her fleet of nimble servants choose to ignore, or were they unaware of the belief that it is unlucky to bring lilac into the house? That it is a flower of death, and pre-sages disaster? Lilac flowers were dropped on the coffins of those who died in May, and Walt Whitman wrote of the death of President Lincoln:

> With the tolling tolling bells' perpetual clang,
> Here, coffin that slowly passes,
> I give you my sprig of lilac.

But contrariwise, and in the way of flower lore, no May bride should be without it; and for Hazel Woodus, the ill-

117

fated bride in *Gone to Earth*, the whip of the pony cart taking
her to her wedding with Edward Marston, was trimmed with
lilac. In Hazel's sad case, the lilac did indeed foretell disaster.
Although in the *Language of Flowers* the lilac symbolizes the
first emotions of love, it may be safer to avoid it, for in some
country districts, if a lover offered his lass a branch of lilac it
meant that their engagement would be broken off. They are clan-
nish shrubs too, and if you cut a lilac down in your garden, the
others may show their displeasure by failing to bloom next year.

This bush, that seems to us so essentially English, came
originally from China, Persia, and the North Balkan Peninsula;
arriving in Vienna by way of Turkey. John Tradescant the
elder grew it in his garden in South Lambeth in 1640, and
Sir Thomas Hanmer cultivated three varieties in 1659, the
common blue, the rare white, and the red, the rarest of all. At
about the same time, American gardeners were planting lilac
in the gardens of New Hampshire and New Amsterdam.

> The lilac, various in array – now white,
> Now sanguine, and her beauteous head now set
> With purple spikes pyramidal; as if
> Studious of ornament, yet unresolved
> Which hue she most approved, she chose them all.[3]

The complicated confusion of names, whereby the flower we
know as lilac is really Syringa, and the flower we know as
syringa is really Philadelphus, arose from the fact that Gerard
called the purple lilac 'Syringa, the blew Pipe Tree, because
its stems, when the pith is removed, are hollow like a pipe';
and the mock orange, or philadelphus, he called 'the White
Pipe Tree', so that when a white form of lilac was introduced,
it was given the same name, thereby causing confusion and
rancour for generations to come. Country people avoid all
these unnecessary complications by calling it Laylock, Lelaps,
Lily-oak, Mayflower and Ducksbill (because of the rolled
edges of the flowerets).

But Horace Walpole loved both lilac and syringa. He could

scarcely be torn for a day from Strawberry Hill when it was in its 'lilac-tide and seringahood'.

John Drinkwater, too, wrote of the lilac's connection with love and death.

> The lilacs offer beauty to the sun,
> Throbbing with wonder as eternally
> For sad and happy lovers they have done
> With the first bloom of summer in the sky,
> Yet they are newly spread in honour now
> Because, for every beam of beauty given
> Out of that clustering heart, back to the bough,
> My love goes beating, from a greater heaven.
> So be my love for good or sorry luck
> Bound, it has virtue on this April eve
> That shall be there for ever when they pluck
> Lilacs for love. And though I come to grieve
> Long at a frosty tomb, there still shall be
> My happy lyric in the lilac tree.

Most poets agree about the friendly domesticity of the lilac.

> Now you are a very decent flower,
> A reticent flower,
> A curiously clear-cut flower,
> Standing beside clean doorways,
> Friendly to a house-cat and a pair of spectacles,
> Making poetry out of a bit of moonlight
> And a hundred or two sharp blossoms. [4]

I do not know whether Elizabeth's German house still stands, nor whether the lilacs still bloom in her garden; but these last four poignant lines, as sad and as happy as life is, she might share with the unknown Lydia, for they bring garden and house together, as Elizabeth did.

> Lydia is gone this many a year,
>   Yet when the lilacs stir,
> In the old gardens far and near,
>   This house is full of her. [5]

Ranunculus

Ranunculus   I am dazzled by your charms

Poets are shy of the ranunculus. It is a charming flower, but it cannot be fitted neatly into verse. A ranunculus by any other name would sound a great deal sweeter, even though it doesn't smell at all. If any fairy godmother were invited to its christening, it must have been the bad one, for its name means 'Little Frog', because in its wild state it was thought to grow in places frequented by frogs. Nor has it gathered to itself many pet names in its journey through Asia to Europe. Not, that is, until it finally settled in England, brought in the pockets of the Huguenots, to whom gardeners owe so many lovely plants, when some kindly cultivator called it Fair Maid of France. But this pleasant name did not stick, and ranunculus it is and will ever be, which is why

> Poets seldom make a fuss
> About the poor ranunculus.

There is one other ancient name that should be mentioned here, but it is not one that is likely to help the case of this ill-fated flower. At one time it was called Strumea, because it was used as a cure for a complaint known as strumae, which was similar to the King's Evil. The green leaves could be used to lay upon blisters, and the root was chewed to relieve tooth-ache. One kind produced a poison that was used on the tips of arrows.

Growing wild in Persia and Turkey, it became a much prized flower in the Imperial Gardens of the Seraglio in Constantinople, whence it passed to France and Holland. In due course it arrived in England. Clusius grew it in his garden, for Gerard said that 'he received a plant fresh and greene, the which a domesticall theefe stole foorth of his garden.'

By the end of the eighteenth century there were at least eight hundred varieties, for the seed never produces two flowers alike, and it was in these varieties that the nurserymen endeavoured to make up for the injustice done earlier, by giving them the names of famous men. 'I was acquainted with a Set of Florists, who began to dignify each new Ranunculus with the Name of some Person of distinguished Merit. One was called King Stanislaus, and another the Czarina: a third was Marshal Villars, and a fourth Prince Eugene. . . . But our Florists soon discontinued this Practice, for when they compared the Number of Great Men, with the Diversity of these Flowers that were daily making their Appearance, they grew sensible that the Generality of them would be in Danger of continuing nameless.'[1]

During this fruitful period Thomas Hogg, a successful florist of Paddington Green, gave a description of their colouring which gives a slight idea of what we now miss in our indifference: 'A bed of fine Ranunculuses is esteemed by many, in no degree inferior to a bed of the richest Tulips. Here yellow globular blossoms present themselves in all shades, from the pale straw to the golden crocus; red of all tints — pink, rose, and flame colour; purple and crimson of every dye; black, brown, olive, and violet, of every hue. Besides these, there are yellow spotted flowers, brown spotted and white spotted, red and purple streaked, red and white striped, red and yellow striped, besides mottled and bridled in countless varieties.'

Later in the book he remarks peevishly of his competitors in Holland, 'Many persons are fond of buying Dutch Ranunculuses and Tulips, which now come over every autumn, under the impression of not only getting them very cheap (which of course they sometimes are enabled to do, as it would not answer the importer's purpose to send them back again to Holland unsold) but also of getting them very fine. In this they are not seldom disappointed, for the Dutchman is something like the Jew in his dealing: you must not expect great bargains for little money; he is very seldom charged, I believe, with sending us any of his best flowers among his common mixtures: his Pell Mells, as the florists call them, are upon the whole very indifferent, and not worth the amateur's notice.'[2]

What was the cause of such a rise and fall such as this, that could provoke the comment, in 1909, 'a flower not often to be met with in quantity in England, where it is not popular. Why, is not clear, certainly one might have thought it old fashioned enough to have returned to favour with straight-backed chairs and china dogs and cottage ornaments.'[3]

The china dogs are still well ahead in popularity, and it is time we demanded the return of these spotted, streaked and bridled varieties that could add such interest to our gardens. But at least it is pleasant to know that this unfortunate Frog Flower once played a modest part in an experiment made by the great Linnaeus, even though it is a story without an end. On one of his scientific expeditions, hearing his secretary describing the incredible powers of the divining rod, Linnaeus buried a purse containing a hundred ducats under a ranunculus plant which grew by itself in a meadow, and challenged the secretary to find the purse if he could. The rod discovered nothing, and Linnaeus' ranunculus was trodden underfoot by the searchers, until when he went to fetch the purse he was unable to find it. The diviner went to his assistance, and after telling Linnaeus that he was going in quite the wrong direction, the rod eventually indicated the whereabouts of the buried treasure. Linnaeus went so far as to admit that another such experiment would convince him, but whether another experiment took place, or whether in the cause of scientific enquiry the Frog Flower died a martyr's death, to no avail, we are not told. It probably did.

Clematis

Our native species, *C. vitalba*, was first called Traveller's Joy
by Gerard. At that time it was commonly known as Hedge-
vine, or Viorna, from *vias ornans*, which meant 'adorning the
ways and hedgerows'. Another name of the period was Love.
'The Gentlewimen call it Love, but Gerard coyned that name
of Travellerrs joy . . . the leaves are of a sleepie property,
smelling like unto Nightshade, having withall peradventure
some deleteriall or deadly quality in them also, because flies
resting on them were extinguished or kild.'[1]

In 1569 Hugh Morgan, apothecary to Queen Elizabeth I,
grew a species which he had obtained from abroad, *C. viticella*;
and by 1597 two varieties, a blue and a red, were cultivated in
English gardens. Tradition says that this climber, known as
Ladies' or Virgin's Bower, sheltered Our Lady during the
flight from Egypt, and under this name it is dedicated to the
Feast of the Assumption, 15 August.

> When Mary left us here below,
> The Virgin's Bower began to blow.[2]

Others believe it to have been so called in honour of the
Virgin Queen, but this is unlikely, as it was known in France as
Le Berceau de Vierge before the reign of Elizabeth I.

Thomas Hanmer, the close friend of John Evelyn, grew
three varieties in his garden at Bettisfield; 'The single with the
red flower: The blew or purple as some call it with the single
flower: And the dowble darke blew or purple.'[3]

By 1785 still only four small-flowered kinds were known,
and it was not until the middle of the nineteenth century that
the large-flowered clematis was beginning to appear. Since

123

then, the clematis grows from strength to strength and beauty to beauty.

In 1629 Parkinson had heard of a double white clematis. 'I have been informed from some of my especiall friends that they have a double white Clematis, and have promised to send it, but whether it will be of the climing or upright sort, I cannot tell untill I see it: but surely I doe much doubt whether the double will give any good seede.'

Gerard, remarkably for him, could not find any medicinal use for this climbing member of the buttercup family. 'These plants have no use in physicke as yet found out, but are esteemed only for pleasure, by reason of the goodly shadow which they make with their thicke bushing and clyming, as also for the beauty of the flowers, — the pleasant sent or savour of the same.'

But the waste-not want-not French, made pickles from the young shoots and baskets from the stripped bark. They also used the shoots to tie up young trees. English country lads cut short lengths of the woody stems which they lighted at one end and smoked, hence the rural names of Smoking Cane, Shepherd's Delight, Smoke Wood, Tom-Bacca and Devil's Cut. Kipling called it Hot-wood, which seems to be a reference to the same use. In Germany, too, clematis pipes were smoked, and there they were called Devil's Band or Devil's Thread, probably because of its tangled seed heads. At various times these seeds have been used in the making of paper, but this has proved too brittle for complete success. But the harvest mice have found a most satisfactory use for the soft grey down of the ripened seed head. Stripping off small feathery tufts they make themselves little nests like the nests of birds, in which to spend the winter.

The juice of the root when applied to the skin causes ulcers, and this was once used by beggars, in order to gain pity. When used too often, it could cause real and permanent wounds.

The beautiful cultivated flowers of the present age do not seem to appeal to the poets, but the Old Man's Beard, other-

wise known as Grandfather's Whiskers, that cloaks the hedges
outside the cottage garden is the true joy of the countryman.
John Clare wrote of

> — the very spot,
> Just where the old man's beard all wildly trails
> Rude arbours o'er the road, and stops the way — [4]

and Gilbert White notes in his *Journal* for 23 November 1788
that 'the downy seeds of traveller's joy fill the air, and driving
before a gale, appear like insects on the wing.'

The poet Edward Thomas likens the beard to smoke:

> The smoke of traveller's joy is puffed
> Over hawthorn berry and hazel tuft.

That the plain and sensitive Mary Ann Evans, later to gain
fame as the novelist, George Eliot, could ever have been
known to the romantic girl friends of her youth as 'Clematis',
comes as a surprise. But the sentimental *Language of Flowers*
seems to have been accepted without question, even by such a
young intellectual as Mary Ann, or Marian, as she preferred
to be called. She wrote to a friend, 'You must know I have had
bestowed on me the very pretty cognomen of Clematis, which,
in the floral language, means mental beauty. I cannot find it in
my heart to refuse it, though . . . it has RATHER the appearance of a satire than a compliment.'[5]

Did she ever blush at the memory of 'Clematis', when she
became known to the literary world as George?

And the final word on the subject of its pronunciation comes
from Stanley Whitehead's book, *Garden Clematis*, in a verse by
J. E. Spingarn:

> Because it climbs on lattice,
> The rabble says Cle — ma — tis,
> But Webster will not cease to hiss
> Until they call it Clem — a — tis.

Carnation

Lively and pure affection

I confess to having a slight prejudice against greenhouse carnations. They are too beautifully perfect; too perfectly beautiful. One prize red bloom is precisely the same as the next prize red bloom; one long-stemmed pink one, identical with its neighbour. They have no expression.

This does not happen with other flowers. A perfect rose of any variety is not the identical twin of another of the same breed; an inner petal curves with a fuller pout, an outer one expands more widely, or there is a deeper flush at its base. A carnation never looks worried as some pansies do, or blowsy like a poppy, or contemplative like a lily of the valley, or slightly impudent like its close relative, the Sweet William. But given half a dozen perfect carnations, with whatever careless art you may arrange them, they will defy you by looking like six pretty girls emerging immaculate from the hairdresser's with identical shampoos and sets.

As it happens, my analogy is not so far out, for Christopher Nunn, a barber and hairdresser of Enfield in the eighteenth century, was noted for his skill in dressing carnations and pinks for prize exhibition, and at certain times of year he had as many applications to dress carnations as he had to dress wigs. He also made the useful discovery that his old and outmoded wigs, full of human grease as they were, made excellent compost.

In the interests of justice, however, I must now hasten to give you other opinions of the carnation, which will not, I promise you, be at all the same as mine. Take William Cobbett's, for instance. 'Some persons may think that flowers are things of no use, that they are nonsensical things. The same may be, and, perhaps with more reason, said of pictures.

126

An Italian, while he gives his fortune for a picture, will laugh to scorn an Hollander, who leaves a tulip-root as a fortune to his son. For my part, as a thing to keep, and not to sell; as a thing, the possession of which is to give me pleasure, I hesitate not a moment to prefer the plant of a fine Carnation to a gold watch set with diamonds.'[1]

Or this from John Rea:

> For various colours Tulips most excel,
> And some Anemonies do please as well:
> Ranunculus in richest scarlets shine,
> And Bear's Ears may with these in beautie joyn:
> But yet if ask and have were in my power,
> Next to the Rose give me the Gilliflower.

This name gillyflower, shared with both wallflower and stock, may, in the case of the carnation, have come from girofle, a clove, and because of its strong scent, 'the dusky, dark, carnation breath of clove,'[2] was often called the clove gillyflower to mark it from the others. Its other name, carnation or coronation, came from its use at festivals in wreaths and garlands. Because of its clove scent, it was often dropped into wine, to give it 'bouquet', and known as sops-in-wine. Mary, the estranged young wife of Milton, wrote in her diary of 23 June 1644, how she 'was in the Garden, gathering a few Coronations and Sops-in-Wine, and thinking they were of a deeper crimson at Sheepscote', where her friend Rose Agnew lived.

Not everyone likes this rather heavy scent. Reginald Farrer the Alpine plant collector, called it 'decadent', but to me the flowers have that slightly dusty smell of artificial flowers on a Victorian bonnet, or the *papier poudre* that our mothers allowed us to use to 'clean up' on a journey.

'For its beauty it is admitted into the gardens of the curious. . . . The beauties of this plant in its wild state were too conspicuous to escape the notice of the florists, who, by their unwearied attention to its culture, have raised from it all that vast and beautiful variety of carnations which they justly esteem the pride of their gardens. . . . There is a syrup of them kept in the shops, but it is too much loaded with sugar to be of any use. Perhaps the best preparation of them is a strong tincture with brandy.'[3]

Perhaps it is.

The carnation was unknown to the Greeks and Romans until in the time of Caesar Augustus it was found in Spain, where it was also used to spice drinks. It may have reached England during the Roman occupation. Another theory is that it came to this country during the Norman Conquest, possibly with the stones imported for building. At all events, the wild plant from which the garden varieties were developed was a great frequenter of castles, and became naturalized on Rochester Castle, and the other Norman castles of Dover, Ludlow and Deal.

'A gimp and gallant flower,' Walter de la Mare calls it, 'the chiefest of account in Tudor gardens.'[4] By 1700, three hundred and sixty kinds and four classes of clove gillyflower, the Flake, the Bizarre, the Piquette or picottee and the Painted Lady, the last now gone. The Flake was striped; the Bizarre was composed of a fantastic mixture of not less than three shades, and Picottees had coloured edges or were mottled and spotted. Yellow picottees were grown by the Empress Josephine in her garden at Malmaison. Queen Charlotte also had a superb collection, sent to her from Germany.

Gallant names they bore, too, such as Master Bradshawe, his dainty Lady; John Wittie, his great Tawnie Gilloflour; The Fair Maid of Kent, and Master Tuggie's Princess. Master Tuggie must have died before his wife, because we read of carnations being called Tuggies, after Mistress Tuggie of Westminster, who had a wonderful collection. Another memorable name was Snook's Defiance — could this be the snook-cocking Snook, and did he cock one at all the less successful carnation growers?

Gerard also grew a yellow carnation, 'The which a worshipfull merchant of London, Master Nicholas Lete, procured from Poland, and gave me thereof for my garden, which before that time was never seene nor heard of in these countries.'

So great was the skill and care lavished on them by the florists that Sir Herbert Maxwell remarked in 1908 that 'a wild mother carnation could not recognize her own offspring in the monstrous Malmaison race (unless it were by scent, as a ewe does her lamb).'[5]

The popularity of the carnation reached its height in the reign of Charles I, but during the Civil War it was almost lost to our gardens. In Charles II's reign they were brought back from Holland and restarted, although they were not so hardy as before.

A gillyflower instead of a peppercorn was sometimes paid as a nominal rent, in acknowledgement that the tenement belonged to the receiver of the flower.

'Lands and tenements in Ham, Surrey, were formerly held by John of Handloo of the men of Kingston on condition of rendering to the said men three Clove gilliflowers at the king's coronation. A clove gilliflower when any King or Queen is crowned at the castle of Berkhampstead.'[6] This would have been the small clove-scented single flower, and three hundred years ago this sort of entry in the records was not uncommon.

In France and parts of Italy, 29 June is called Carnation Day, and dedicated to St Peter and St Paul, and the carnation has also become the emblem of Mother's Day in America, held on the second Sunday in May; and so

>   – this flow'r exacts our care;
> For if th' extremes of heat or cold the air
> Molest too much, they're blasted in their birth,
> Unable to aspire above the earth.
> Morning and evening therefore you must chuse
> To water them, or else their charms they lose.[7]

Pink

Dianthus

Since each colour has a different meaning in *The Language of Flowers* if you don't want to put a foot wrong, it is best to regard the pink as 'an emblem of love'.

I have a book of Elizabethan verse pleasantly entitled, *A Poesie of Gilloflowers, eche differing from other in Colour and Odour, yet all sweete*, and although this is in reference to the poems it contains, yet it makes a very suitable introduction to this cottage garden flower. Humble it may be, but as a flower as well as a synonym, it is the very pink of perfection, clear coloured, with petals roundly cut or neatly jagged like the jerkin of a court jester.

Simple to grow, the pink is yet worth studying, as that grand old man of gardening, Fred Streeter, evidently found, when he fell from a window at the age of two into a bed of them, and started thus suddenly on a horticultural career.

Its family name comes from *Dios*, a god, and *anthos*, a flower, and so it is the flower of the Gods. Up to the sixteenth century the pink was invariably a single flower. 'The Pynkes and small feathered Gillofers are like to the double or clove Gillofers in leaves, stalkes, and floures, saving they be single and a great deal smaller . . . with five or six small leaves, deep and finely snipt, or fringed like to small feathers of white, redde, and carnation colour.'[1]

But something about this well-tempered plant especially appealed to the Paisley florists and the artisans of the north country. If Lancelot Brown had been a florist instead of a landscape gardener, he would doubtless have been struck with the 'capabilities' of the pink, but Brown was no flower lover, and, in any case, the weavers and colliers were already

PLATE V

Honeysuckle

Hand-coloured engraving by William Clark, engraver to
the London Horticultural Society, from *The Moral of
Flowers*, Mrs. Hey, 1835.

Carnations

1 Emperor. 2 Jenny Lind. 3 Duke of Devonshire

PLATE VI

Three Carnations
Emperor, Jenny Lind and Duke of Devonshire

Drawn and engraved by T. Rosenberg, from *The Florists'*
Guide, 1850.

busy with its cultivation, which they carried out with great care and to their own self-imposed standards. So carefully nurtured were they that neat little umbrellas of tin were made to shelter them.

The Floricultural Cabinet of 1841 gives something of the early history of the pink. 'The first Pink worthy of notice was raised in the year 1772 by Mr. James Major, who was then gardener to the Duchess of Lancaster; previous to which there were but four sorts, and those of very little note, being cultivated only for common border flowers. Mr. Major having saved some seed in 1771, he reared several plants, which, blooming the next season, one out of the number proved to be a double flower with laced petals, at which he was agreeably surprised. He later sold these at 10s. 6d. a pair, under the name of Major's Duchess of Lancaster, the orders for which amounted to £80. This was in Lewisham, Kent, where Mr. Major died in 1831 at the age of ninety-four.'[2]

Since symbols play such an important part in flower lore, the pink should be made the emblem of Everyman, for not only was it the Poorman's darling, as in John Clare's:

> A path with Pinks and Daisies trimm'd
> Led from the homely entrance gate;
> The door, worm-eaten and decay'd,
> Bespoke the tenants low estate,

but it was cultivated by kings and princes too. Henry IV of Provence first brought it to the gardens of France, and Prince Condé, Louis II of Bourbon, known as the Grand Condé, when imprisoned at Vincennes, cheered his long hours of captivity with their culture; until, after being condemned as a traitor by the Parliament of Paris, he finally was pardoned in 1659.

In contrast to the neat and decorous 'laced' pink, the well-known Mrs Sinkins, that gloriously scented white beauty that bursts her 'podds' and flops all over our garden paths, might be called an 'unlaced' pink, yet in spite of this indiscipline, she is the best known of them all. Alice Coats, who has a vast knowledge of garden history, gives her rags-to-riches story. Raised in a workhouse garden by the Master of Slough Poor Law Institution, she was named in honour of his wife, and so great was her success, that when in 1938 Slough became a borough, the Mrs Sinkins pink was incorporated in its coat of arms. There's glory for you.

The stiff little pink or carnation held in the hand of a young man or woman in many old portraits, is a sign of their recent betrothal. The portrait itself was probably painted to mark the occasion that the flower symbolizes.

Flowers come and flowers go, but 'as pretty as a pink' still remains as neat a compliment to a young girl as she could wish.

> And 'clipping pinks' (which maiden's Sunday gowns
> Full often wear catcht at by toying chaps)
> Pink as the ribbons round their snowy caps.[3]

Sweet William

Gallantry, finesse and perfection

'These kindes of flowers as they come nearest unto Pinkes and Gilloflowers though manifestly differing, so it is fittest to place them next unto them in a peculiar chapter.'[1]

Like a miniature bouquet of pinks on one stalk, Sweet Williams were 'kept and maintained in gardens more for to please the eie, than either the nose or the belly,'[2] and so they are today. They cannot be without perfume, however, or why should they be called 'Sweet', and Matthew Arnold wrote of them as 'Sweet Williams with their homely cottage smell'.

'They are not used either in meat or medicine, but esteemed for their beauty to decke up gardens, the bosomes of the beautifull, garlands and crownes for pleasure.'[1] Those same bosoms, presumably, on which fritillaries had rested earlier in the year.

Sweet Williams, Velvet Williams, Bloomydowns and London Tuftes, as they were variously called, are a species of pink, *D. barbatus*, the 'bearded' pink. In Wales they are known as Sweet Evanses.

The 'London Tufts of many a mottled hue', had been mentioned by Parkinson, and in the same paragraph he includes London Pride, 'but the speckled kinde is termed by our English Gentlewomen, for the most part, London Pride,' but the London Pride that we know is a saxifrage, and unrelated to Sweet William. The Dutch call them Keykens, 'as though you should say a bundell of cluster or flowers for in their vulgar tongue bundells or flowers or nosegaies they call Keykens.'[2]

They were common in gardens in Gerard's day, and much loved by country people for buttonholes and bough-pots. Mary Webb, describing an harvest home writes of oxen bedecked with thick chains of Sweet Williams and Travellers' Joy and Corn.

But by 1879 the Reverend Henry Bright was writing, 'This dear old Sweet William, which was the favourite in old cottage gardens, and which, with the Lad's-love and the Pink, was the chosen flower for the buttonhole of the country boy, is now far too much neglected.'[3]

The origin of its name remains a mystery. The flower was probably raised from the small red pink found wild near Rochester, originally called Saint Sweet-William, and dedicated to St William of Rochester, whose day is 25 June. This is only conjecture because the 'Saint' was dropped after the demolition of St William's shrine in the Cathedral.

However, as there are at least seven St Williams, including St William of Rochester, already mentioned; St William of Norwich; St William of Montpelier, and St William of Aquitaine, any of these worthies might have claimed the flower as his own.

St William of York, who died in 1154, has his day on 8 June. He was Archbishop of York, and miracles attributed to him are shown in the windows of the Minster.

St William of Norwich died in 1144, and his day is 26 March. He was martyred as a boy, in a wood outside Norwich, and he is portrayed on the rood-screen at Worstead and in Lodden, Norfolk.

It is hardly likely to have been St William of Montpelier, for he is depicted with a lily growing out of his mouth.

St William of Aquitaine, who died in 812, was half soldier and half monk. Because of his popularity throughout southern Europe he could well have been the Sweet William we are seeking, but the flower originally came from Germany, and we are left without a clue.

So let us not neglect this rather sprawly but bright-complexioned plant, and let us cultivate good Sweet-Saint-William, whoever he may be — perhaps he will put in a good word for us later on.

Marigold

Calendula   Jealousy

No Poorman's Nosegay, not to mention his garden, can be
complete without the marigold. With its honest round face,
slightly shiny, like the face of a cheerful cook – and indeed, it
had a place as a pot- or salad-herb in most Tudor kitchens – it
is hard to imagine why it should be regarded as the emblem of
jealousy.

Both Chaucer and Herrick write of it as the flower of
jealousy. The figure of jealousy is described by Chaucer as
wreathed with marigolds; and Herrick, in 'How Marigolds
Came Yellow,' says:

> Jealous Girles these sometimes were,
> While they liv'd, or lasted here:
> Turn'd to Flowers, still they be
> Yellow, markt for Jealousie.

Much as I love those two poets, I cannot believe that the
marigold shows the green tinge of jealousy. The greenish
sulphur pallor of the primrose would serve much better as an
emblem of a jealous maiden. While on this subject of colour,
there is a strange story of Linnaeus' daughter who observed
in the flowers a curious electrical phenomenon. Towards the
close of the hot days of July and August, at sunset, when the
atmosphere was clear, she saw flashes of light coming from
the marigold flowers. Being the daughter of a scientist, and
not just a superstitious country lass, this had to be taken
seriously. But it was not a figment of her imagination. These
flashes, lasting for about half an hour, have been described by
later witnesses. Darwin mentions a Mr Haggren, who, in
order to prove to himself that this was no deception of the eye,
placed a man near him with orders to make a signal at the mo-

ment when he observed the light. They both saw it constantly at the same time. The light was most brilliant on marigolds of an orange or flame colour. Light flashes have also been observed coming from sunflowers, nasturtiums, orange lilies and African marigolds, but only in flowers of bright gold or orange, and never on damp, rainy days.

C. officinalis, the garden marigold, 'is an herbe called ruddes. . . . It . . . groweth most in gardens and numerous places. Maydens make garlands of it when they go to feestes and brydeales because it hath fair yellowe flowers and ruddy. And it is called Calendula because it beareth flowres all the kalends of every month of the yeare.'[1] The maydens must have had to hurry home from their feestes and brydeales like so many Cinderellas, for the flowers closed promptly at three o'clock, after which the maydens must have presented a somewhat shabby appearance. It opens, according to Linnaeus, from nine in the morning, and because of its regular hours of duty he grew it in his Horologium Florae. For this reason it was called the Husbandman's Dyall. 'These Flowers are the true Clients of the Sunne; how observant they are of his motion and influence. At even they shut up, as mourning for his departure, without whom they neither can nor would flourish; in the morning they welcome his rising with a cheerful open-nesse, and at noone, are fully display'd in a free acknowledgment of his bounty.'[2] Keats wrote of the morning wakening of the marigolds,

> Open afresh your round of starry folds,
> Ye ardent marigolds!
> Dry up the moisture from your golden lids,
> For great Apollo bids
> That in these days your praises should be sung
> On many harps, which he hath lately strung.

Gerard says that 'the yellow leaves of the floures are dried and kept throughout Dutchland against Winter, to put into broth in Physicall potions, and for divers other purposes, in such quantity, that in some Grocers or Spice-sellers houses are to be found barrells filled with them, and retailed by the penny more or lesse, insomuch that no broths are well made without dried Marigolds.'

It would seem that they were not to everyone's taste however. Charles Lamb, remembering the unappetizing menus of Christ's Hospital when he was a scholar there, speaks with distaste of 'boiled beef on Thursdays . . . with detestable marigolds floating in the pail to poison the broth.'[3]

Single flowers were more popular for both medicinal and culinary purposes than double ones. Philip Miller, author of *The Gardeners' Dictionary*, and Gardener to the Worshipful Company of Apothecaries at their Botanic Garden at Chelsea, says that they are to be preferred, 'having a much better Scent, and add a stronger flavour to the Soups,' and Cobbett agrees, adding, 'The double one is an ornamental flower, and a very mean one indeed.' A stinking mini Wen, perhaps?

To W. H. Hudson the marigold appears not as a cheerful cook nor as a jealous maiden, but as something remote and very beautiful. 'How the townsman, town born and bred, regards this flower I do not know. He is, in spite of all the time I have spent in his company, a comparative stranger . . . a pale people with hurrying feet and eager, restless minds, who live apart in monstrous crowded camps. . . . What, then, does it matter how they regard this common orange-coloured flower with a strong smell? For me it has an atmosphere, a sense or suggestion of something immeasurably remote and very beautiful . . . an event, a place, a dream perhaps, which has left no distinct image, but only this feeling unlike all others, imperishable, and not to be described except by the one word Marigold.'[4]

But perhaps the saddest lines ever written on the marigold were by Charles I, during his imprisonment in Carisbrooke Castle.

> The marigold observes the Sun
> More than my Subjects me have done.[5]

Hollyhock

Female Ambition (to be
                                    the tallest plant in the garden?)

Steeples of chalky bloom overlooking garden fences, always
pictured, although not mentioned, in Contrary Mary's garden.

Many flowers have been brought into our gardens from the
wild, but Henry Phillips, a nineteenth-century flower historian,
suggested that the hollyhock, the only landscape flower that
we possess, 'should be planted among the hedges of the
countryside, partly to relieve the uniformity of the fields, and
partly to extend the honey-gathering season of the bees.'[1]
He says also that a good strong cloth could be made from the
fibrous bark of the flower stalks; and in the year 1821 about
two hundred and eighty acres of land near Flint, in Wales,
were planted with hollyhocks, with the intention of converting
the fibres into thread similar to flax or hemp. It must have
been a charming sight; a pastel parade ground. During the
manufacture it was discovered that the plants yielded a fine
blue dye, equal in beauty and permanence, he says, to the best
indigo. No more was heard of this experiment, which is a
pity. We could do with more hollyhock fields, even though
we may not welcome a homespun hollyhock appearance ourselves.

'Of the garden mallow called hollihocke,' wrote Gerard,
'The tame or garden mallow bringeth forth broad leaves of a
whitish greene colour, rough and greater than those of the
wild mallow . . . now and then of a deep purple colour, varying
diversely as Nature list to play with it: in their places groweth
up a round knop like a little cake, compact or made of a
multitude of flat seeds like little cheeses. . . . The Hollihoke
is called of divers, Rosa ultra-marina or outlandish Rose.'

Early in the nineteenth century it gained the rank of

florists' flower, although never one of the most popular. Wordsworth grew them in his garden, and his avenues of hollyhocks were the pride of Rydal.

It is a landscape flower, 'the only landscape flower we possess — the only one, that is, whose forms and colours tell in the distance; and so picturesque is it, that perhaps no artist ever attempted to draw a garden without introducing it, whether it was really there or not. By far the finest effect that combined art and nature ever produced in gardening, were those fine masses of many-coloured hollyhocks clustered round a weather-tinted vase, such as Sir Joshua delighted to place in the wings of his pictures.'[2]

A common plant in England since 1440, it was known and loved in even earlier times in China, where the petals were used in cookery. For the Chinese it is a symbol of Nature and Fecundity, perhaps, after all, the Female Ambition of our Language of Flowers.

Maeterlinck describes the hollyhock as 'riding her high horse and flaunting her silky cockades,'[3] but the higher the rise, the farther the fall, and her end is a sorry one.

> Who bids the hollyhock uplift
> Her rod of fast-sealed buds on high;
> Fling wide her petals — silent, swift,
> Lovely to the sky?
> Since as she kindled, so she will fade,
> Flower upon flower in squalor laid.[4]

Snapdragon

I have always thought that every snapdragon, whatever its colour, resembles somebody's old aunt; that it is, indeed, a sort of Charlie's Aunt of flowers. I suppose it is the combination of velvet bonnet and jutting underlip; although I am aware that few people's old aunts look like that any more. It seems as though there are others who share this feeling, for in 1860 James Andrews wrote in a nice little book *Choice Garden Flowers*: 'There is an old picture representing the human face divine of a man and a woman, both smirking and smiling when held in one position, and inscribed below with the words "before marriage"; if we turn the picture round so that the top becomes the bottom, we still observe two faces, but the expression of each is grim and sour, and below are the expressive words "after marriage". These faces, especially when held in the latter position, always remind one of the Snapdragon.'

Walter de la Mare noticed this human appearance too, and describes a luncheon party where Lady Diana Templeton 'smiled like a mauve-pink snapdragon'.[1]

There are two British species of old aunts, the great snapdragon, which grows on walls and chalk hills, probably the outcast of the neighbouring gardens, and the small snapdragon, which grows in sandy fields. In its eagerness for an aristocratic address the great snapdragon stakes its claim on castle walls even before ruin sets in, like a vulture waiting for its intended prey. 'Berkeley Castle, which though not at all ruinous, and with walls that look as strong and closely built as they ever were, is almost covered in many places with red, white and yellow snapdragons. I recollect remarking when there, that the old keep looked like a hanging garden, it was so gaily broidered over with bright-tinted flowers.'[2]

It can be regarded as a true cottage plant, 'a rustic rather than an elegant plant',[3] and its names of Dog's Mouth, Lion's Snap, Toad's Mouth and Bull-dog's Mouth have a rustic ring about them. Even its seeds seem animal rather than vegetable, and Gerard says 'in mine opinion it is more like unto the bones of a sheep's head that hath been long in the water, or the flesh consumed clean away'. Hung round the neck, the plant was reported to have the power to destroy charms.

During the nineteenth century it was raised to the status of florists' flower, with a list of rules by which it, and its breeder, must abide. In Russia it was sown for its seed, which produces an oil little inferior to that obtained from olives.

D. H. Lawrence's poem, 'Snapdragon', is an all-or-nothing poem. One cannot quote a part of it, but if you want to see deeper into the crimson throat of this strange yet common flower than you have ever seen before, this is the poem to read.

De la Mare has a story of an unhappy gardener in the Island of Rumm, who without ill intent called a snapdragon an antirrhinum: 'And there arose out of the hillside a Monster named Zobj —'[4], but I can't tell you any more, because that is as far as De la Mare goes. However

> A snapdragon grew in the Island of Rumm,
> It was called by a gardener Anti-rrhi-num.
> Now the man may have had a green finger AND thumb
> But he blighted the life of that flower of Rumm,
> For you cannot be happy AND Anti-rrhi-num!

My mother, who was a law unto herself in such matters, solved the whole problem with her usual sweeping simplicity. She called it an-tirrium, and everybody seemed to know what she meant. Try it, and see if it isn't a lot better.

Cardinal Newman wrote a touching account of his departure from Oxford in 1846. 'I took leave of my first college, Trinity, which was so dear to me . . . Trinity had never been unkind to me. There used to be much snapdragon growing on the walls opposite my freshman's rooms there, and I had for years taken it as the emblem of my own perpetual residence, even unto death, in my University.'

Today we have a more glamorous, open-plan type of snap-dragon, a prize-winning pin-up girl, instead of an old aunt. She has discarded her old-fashioned bonnet, and wishes to be known as the penstemmon-flowered antirrhinum, Madame Butterfly. And because the life of a pin-up girl is painfully short, Madame Butterfly is already being supplanted by an even more attractive new-comer, Little Darling.

But still old aunt snapdragon maintains her stubborn hold on the warm red brick of Berkeley Castle, while Little Darling has to be content with a small back garden like mine.

Larkspur and Delphinium

Delphinium   Ardent attachment and lightness

Both larkspur and delphinium share the same name, *Delphinium*, in botanical classification, but there they part company, for the older annual plant was likened to a bird, and called by the various names of Lark's head, Lark's toes, Lark's claw and Larkspur, by which we know it today; and the later perennial was named after a fish, because the bud was thought to resemble a dolphin, 'for the floures, and especially before they be perfected, have a certain shew and likenesse of those Dolphins which old pictures and armes of certain antient families have expressed with a crooked and bending figure or shape'.[1]

The wild larkspur, which is related to both buttercup and columbine, was known as a weed of the cornfields around Cambridgeshire, where it may have escaped from gardens. It is said to have been brought from Siberia in the sixteenth century, and single larkspurs were certainly cultivated in Elizabethan gardens. 'The garden Larks spur hath a round stem ful of branches, set with tender jagged leaves: the floures grow alongst the stalks toward the tops of the branches, of a blew colour, consisting of five little leaves which grow together and make one hollow floure, having a taile or spur at the end turning in like the spur of Todeflax.'[1]

It was not until the beginning of the seventeenth century that double flowers appeared, and these were greatly improved by the Dutch. But with the doubling of the flowers, the spur which had given its name to the larkspur, or sometimes, knightspur, disappeared, and the true delphinium evolved, taller, with thicker heads of blossom, a wider leaf and more branching stems. The earliest known larkspurs were unimpressive: 'Larks heels, or spurs, or toes, as in several

143

Countries they are called, exceed in the variety of colours, both single and double, any of the former times; for until of late dayes none of the most pleasant colours were seen or heard of: but now the single kinds are reasonable well dispersed over the land, yet the double kindes of all those pleasant colours (and some other also are beautiful), which stand like littel double Roses, are enjoyed but of a few: all of them rise from seed, and must be sown every year, the double as well as the single.'[2]

Here we can almost watch these 'littel double Roses,' still annuals, developing into the perennial delphinium; the clear simple colours improving yearly, until blue becomes suffused with lilac, grey, pink and almost midnight blue, and some with splashes of black or brown, like bees who have just settled. Side by side with these, the larkspurs that Maeterlinck called 'the rough larkspur in his peasant's blouse,' improved in size and colour, and in 1855 Jane Loudon mentions a scarlet annual larkspur, *D. cardinalis*, from California, and a Siberian larkspur with a strange metallic lustre as of tarnished silver.

Larkspurs had little use in medicine, and even Gerard, who seemed to believe most tall stories, thought little of them as an antidote for scorpion stings. 'We find little extant of the vertues of Larkes heele, either in the antient or later writers, worth the noting; or to be credited; yet it is set downe, that the seed of Larkes spur drunken is good against the stingings of Scorpions; whose vertues are so forceable, that the herbe onely throwne before the Scorpion or any other venomous beast, couseth them to be without force or strength to hurt, insomuch that they cannot move or stirre until the herbe be taken away: with many other such trifling toys not worth the reading.'[1]

John Clare wrote of

> tall-tufted lark-heels,
> Feather'd thick wi' flowers,[3]

but with the exception of A. A. Milne's classic 'The Dormouse and the Doctor',

There once was a Dormouse who lived in a bed
Of delphiniums (blue) and geraniums (red),
And all the day long he'd a wonderful view
Of geraniums (red) and delphiniums (blue)

delphiniums are seldom to be met with in poetry.

They may, however, achieve immortality of a kind by being dried, and used in winter flower arrangements. If the flowers are cut, stripped of their leaves and placed in a jug three-quarters filled with water, and there left until the water has been absorbed, they may be allowed to dry off in a clean vase, where they will keep their colour for several years, and thus put to shame all faint-hearted poets.

Foxglove

Digitalis   Amiability and confiding love

What is it about freckles that is so appealing? Freckle-faced
boys and freckle-faced cowslips? Freckled eggs and freckled
foxgloves? Boys and cowslips, eggs and foxgloves, are not
half so attractive plain. One might almost say 'a penny plain,
twopence freckled.'

Leonard Fuchs, whose own name was given to the fuchsia,
appears to have been the first writer to call this plant by the
name of *Digitalis*, from the flowers resembling finger-stalls.
According to the naturalist Sowerby, foxglove means Fuch's
glove, but only in so far as Fuchs is German for fox. Other
authorities suggest that the name is a corruption of Fairy
Folks' Gloves, and in various country districts it has answered
to the names of Fairy Bells, Fairy Petticoats, Fairy's Thimbles,
Fairy Fingers, Red Fingers and Our Lady's Glove. In Devon
it was called Flop-top, Flappy-dock and Flop-a-dock, and on
the borders of Dartmoor the children played a game in which
they puffed the bells full of wind to make them go off with a
bang when struck with the hand.

It was first mentioned by Dr Turner in the reign of Queen
Mary. 'There is an herbe that groweth very much in Englande,
and specially in Norfolke, about ye cony holes in sandy
ground, and in divers wooddes, which is called in English
Foxe-gloue. It hath a long stalke, and in the toppe manye
floures hanginge downe like belles or thumbles.'[1]

Possibly our handsomest wild flower, it was early brought
in to the herbarists' gardens and thence to the cottage garden,
when its medicinal properties were discovered. From a cure
for 'slimie flegme and naughtie humours'[2] to a remedy for
the 'King's Evil'; from the healing of wounds to a cure for the
diseases of the heart, there was nothing that the foxglove

PLATE VII

Pink, Violet, Moss Rose and Jasmine

Hand-coloured engraving by James Andrews, from *The
Language, of Flowers or The Pilgrimage of Love*, Thomas
Miller, 1862.

Provence Rose.

London Pub. as the Act directs April 1 1815, by G. Testolini 73 Cornhill.

PLATE VIII

Provence Rose

Hand-coloured engraving from a botanical copybook,
Rudiments of Flower Drawing in Water Colours,
G. Testolini, 1818. (Perhaps the finest of all drawing
books of the period.)

wasn't expected to do, and indeed it is still used in medicine today; although I believe it is no longer true that 'the fox-glove leaf is made into tea, for the sinful purpose of producing intoxication'.[3] However that may be, French apothecaries took it for their symbol, and ornamented their door posts and the piers between their windows with paintings of the flowers.

It was put to a very different use in North Wales a hundred years ago. 'The square stones of the floors are made to look very pretty, being crossed at right angles with two broad black lines, which give to these floors a slight resemblance to mosaic work. This effect is produced by strongly rubbing the stone with a handful of leaves of the foxglove, when the juice dyes this black stain.'[4] It was a weekly process, even throughout the winter, when foxglove leaves could be obtained. This form of decoration, it has been suggested, was less for aesthetic reasons than to ward off the evil eye.

Many writers have loved the foxglove in their youth, and written nostalgically of it in maturity. George Gissing, in *The Private Papers of Henry Rycroft*; George Meredith, in *The Ordeal of Richard Feverel*; and in more recent years, Alison Uttley writes of walking with silky purple gloves and feeling important, 'as if we touched some secret magic.'[5]

But perhaps the foxglove achieved its most sinister role in literature when, in *Precious Bane*, Gideon Sarn poisoned his old mother with foxglove tea.

'Everybody knows as I know nought of yarbs,' said Tivyriah Sexton darkly to Prue Sarn, Gideon's sister. 'Everybody knows Sarn gave the cow foxglove leaves. You and I know that the doctor said your mother seemed as if she'd had foxglove.'[6]

Beverley Nichols endorses the sinister side of this innocent-looking freckled flower. 'I am told that their roots, if boiled and added to the soup, are guaranteed to make your most dis-agreeable enemy expire in considerable discomfort within twenty-four hours, but I have not tested this personally.'[7]

The Scots know it too, for they call it Dead Man's Bells and Bloody Fingers. It was no doubt the favourite flower of

Lady Macbeth. In the precincts of Edinburgh Castle there is a drinking fountain designed by John Duncan to mark the spot where the last of the witches were burned. Two female heads, one full of hate and venom, and the other serene and beautiful; a serpent, standing for both evil and wisdom, and a foxglove flower, for its dual nature of poison and healing, commemorate the martyrdom of the wise women or witches of the superstitious past.

> Within the infant rind of this small flower
> Poison hath residence and medicine power.[8]

Love-in-a-Mist

Nigella   Perplexity and embarrassment

Perhaps the perplexity and embarrassment of *Nigella* arises
from the fact that as St Catherine's flower she has never been
quite sure to which St Catherine she is dedicated. Her problem
is the same as that of Sweet William, and just as there are many
St Williams, so there are several St Catherines. There is St
Catherine of Sienna, whose festival is on 30 April; St Catherine
of Genoa, 14 September, and St Catherine of Alexandria, who
was crushed to death between four spiked wheels rather than
sacrifice to false gods. The Catherine wheel that dizzily rotates
on firework night was certainly named after the third St
Catherine, though her connection with Guy Fawkes is one of
the oddities of folklore. There are St Catherine peaches,
plums and pears that are named in her memory, and so it
seems that although her month of November is against her,
she must claim *Nigella* too, for the wheel of fine fuzzy green
around her bloom.

But to add to her perplexity *Nigella* is torn like St Catherine
herself, between the saint and the devil, because she was also
called Devil-in-a-bush, Devil-in-a-fog, Devil-in-a-mist and
Devil-in-a-frizzle. With the exception of the pansy, never was
flower so bedevilled and befogged with names: Bishop's wort,
Love-entangle, Venus' hair, Spider's claw, Bluebeard, Gith,
Jack-in-prison: Fennel flower, because of her finely cut leaves,
and nigella, for her black seeds.

Maurice Maeterlinck described the drama of her fertiliza-
tion: 'At the source of the flower, the five extremely long
pistils stand close – grouped in the centre of the azure crown,
like five queens clad in green gowns, haughty and inaccessible.
Around them crowd hopelessly the innumerous throng of their
lovers, the stamens which do not come up to their knees. And

now, in the heart of this palace of sapphires and turquoises, in the gladness of the summer days, begins the drama without words or catastrophe which one might expect, the drama of powerless, useless, motionless waiting. But the hours pass that are the flower's years: its brilliancy fades, its petals fall and the pride of the great queens seem at last to bend under the weight of life.'[1]

Gertrude Jekyll did a great deal to improve both colour and size in the variety that is named after her, but the recent Persian Jewels mixture has added rose, carmine, mauve, lavender and purple to the clear blue that Gertrude Jekyll knew and loved.

Cornflower

This flower, a circlet of clear blue, pink, or white darts, accurately surrounding their target, is regarded in *The Language of Flowers* as the emblem of delicacy. I cannot think of any convincing reason for this, as it has a sharpness and a toughness which, with its origin in the cornfields, gives it anything but a delicate air. Perhaps the thought originated with the German ladies, who, according to Anne Pratt, would give them pet names and wear them in their hair, a habit to be discouraged among the over-seventeens, particularly Teutonic over-seventeens.

The flower took the name of centaurea from the legend of the centaur Chiron, who was wounded by an arrow poisoned with the blood of the Hydra. He covered his wound with the blue flowers, and they retained their healing properties from that time.

It is a native British plant, brought into the cottage garden from the cornfields, where it was regarded as the farmers' enemy and known as Hurt-sickle, because its tough stems blunted the reapers' hooks. Culpeper says that 'If you please to take them from the Cornfields and transplant them in your garden, especially towards the full moon, they will grow more double than they are.'[1]

It is seldom seen now in the country, except, of course, in gardens, and there, as Andrew Young says, 'losing the meaning of its name, Cornflower, it also loses half its charm'.[2] Perhaps if gardeners had stuck to the old names of Blue bottle, and its variations of Blue-cup, Blue-bonnet, Blue-blow, and Blue-cap, Andrew Young might have loved it more.

Parkinson, in 1629, also wrote of them as 'furnishing or rather pestering the Corn fieldes', and mentions the garden variety, which 'may most please the delight of our Gentle Florists, in that I labour and strive, to furnish this our garden with the chiefest choyse of natures beauties and delights. . . . We in these dayes do chiefly use them as a cooling Cordiall, and commended by some to be a remedy against not only the plague and pestilentiall diseases, but against the poison of Scorpions and Spiders.'

A good blue ink was obtained from the flowers, and a dye for linen, but the colour was not permanent. In Sowerby's *English Botany* the engraving of the cornflower is coloured with its own juice, but it is much changed. It was also once used by miniaturists in their painting, which is probably the reason why old miniatures are kept in darkened rooms to avoid the action of the sun.

C. Henry Warren, once a broadcaster and writer on country ways, called it 'one of the more elusive weeds of cultivation. Once it has settled in, however,' he said, 'in a habitat obviously suited to its needs, it stays year after year, with an obstinacy that is infuriating to the farmer, but a delight to those who like old favourites turning up in the same place, summer after summer.' He only knew of one locality where the cornflower still grows wild. 'Defying crop rotation and even intensive cultivation, it comes up every year; and every year I go and enjoy the sight of it; but never is it so attractive as when the rotation comes round again to corn. Less tall than the corn stalks, it hides away among the roots, making a rich blue shadow there. One has only to ruffle the corn, however, like stroking a pelt of fur the wrong way, and the flowers will come more boldly into view, thousands of them, a sumptuous blue lining to the ripe corn's cloth of gold.'[3]

It is the emblem of Harrow School.

Poppy

Papaver   Sleep, dreams and fantasy

The packed-to-bursting poppy flower, whether it be the single, scarlet-skirted gipsy of the cornfields, the white-petalled purple-blotched opium poppy, the pale and shivering yellow horned poppy of the sea coast, the black-haired maxi-skirted Oriental houri with the insolent, tatty bearing of a Russell Flint dancer, or the refined and delicate flower bred by the Reverend William Wilks of Shirley, have this in common: that the silky petals retain their creases until they drop, and neither rain nor sun will iron them out.

Many writers have remarked on these silken wrinkles. Alphonse Karr, novelist and one time editor of *Figaro*, wrote: 'Here is a beautiful, rich, and majestic plant. [He must have meant the Oriental poppy.] There is a bud which has risen; tear open its green envelope, and see how its splendid petals are enclosed in it, ragged and without order; you might say it was the carpet bag of a careless student, setting out for the vacation. How can nature treat such fine, rich stuff with so little care?'[1]

The scarlet field poppy is forever linked with battle, for it was from the cornfields of St Martin that John Tradescant, gardener and soldier, fighting the French under Buckingham, brought the first seeds back to England, thereby proving himself no friend to the farmer. Growing in profusion only on cultivated land, the poppy blazed a scarlet trail throughout Europe, running for miles along the straight poplar-lined roads and vineyards of France, and following the Englishmen to Australia with the corn. Now become the emblem of the Great War, it has supplanted the rosemary as the flower of Remembrance.

153

> In Flanders fields the poppies blow
> Between the crosses, row on row.[2]

The artificial poppies sold on Remembrance Day, 11 November, are made by the blind of St Dunstan's, and in 1968 sales reached one and a quarter millions. In 1970, a number of young people brought white poppies to the Cenotaph in Whitehall, as a symbol of Peace, and the generation gap was bridged for one day at least, by white poppies and red.

Not only are the contours of our countryside changing, but the colour is draining from the landscape with the disappearance of cornflower blue and poppy red from our fields. Cobbett mentions 'the Corn-Poppy, which stifles the barley, the wheat and especially the peas, and frequently makes the fields the colour of blood'.[3] But in its battle with the farmers the poppy has been vanquished by chemicals and sprays, until soon the last flame may flicker out, leaving the farm lands richer – and infinitely poorer.

Its story is ancient. Raised by Ceres to console herself for the loss of her daughter Proserpine, who while gathering flowers in the fields of Enna was carried off by Pluto to the Underworld, the poppy was offered up to the Earth-mother, with corn and fruits, in the sacred rites of the Romans. There is a statue of Ceres in the Louvre with wheat and poppies in her hands and hair. Because of this story it is sometimes known as the Red Rose of Ceres. This pagan festival was later incorporated in the Christian calendar, as the feast of St John the Baptist, and poppies and cornflowers became part of the Midsummer day's decorations. It was also dedicated to St Margaret, because, again according to legend, poppies sprang from the blood of the dragon she killed.

> And poppies a sanguine mantle spread
> For the blood of the dragon St. Margaret shed.[4]

Field poppies had many names in the country; Redweed, Cheese-bowl, Corn Rose, Cup-Rose, Windrose, and Headache; the last because its peculiar smell was supposed to cause pains in the head. Another old and attractive name, although I do not know its origin, 'yet our English Gentlewomen in some places call it by a by-name – Joan-Silver-Pin, Fair-without-and-foul-within.'[5] It was also known as Tell-tale, because a petal, crushed in the hand, told whether a lover was true or false; if the petal squeaked he was true, but

> By a prophetic poppy-leaf I found
> Your changed affection, for it gave no sound.
> Though in my hand struck hollow, as it lay,
> But quickly withered, like your love, away.[6]

'The poppy is painted GLASS; it never glows so brightly as when the sun shines through it. Wherever it is seen – against the light or with the light – always it is a flame, and it warms the wind like a blown ruby.'[7] Thus it glowed for Ruskin, and for many another writer.

And thus it glowed for the Countess in *Nature Display'd*, a lady usually so sure of her opinions, but in the case of 'Poppies, or Double Corn-Roses . . . "I am uncertain whether they ought to be considered as a Model, or a Reproach to Painters and Embroiderers" ', she admits.

Poppies have been cultivated in France and Germany for their oily seeds, which are not narcotic, but were used instead of olive oil. A syrup was produced from the petals which was only slightly narcotic, and its juice used for the colouring of medicine. As a dye it is fugitive and unsatisfactory, although it has been used in the making of red ink. The seeds were served with honey in early Roman times, and they are still used to sprinkle on bread.

'I think better of sleep than I ever did, now that she will not easily come near me except in a red hood of poppies,' wrote Elizabeth Barrett to Robert Browning, in May, 1845, but it is the white poppy that is the true poppy of sleep. Brought to Europe from Asia, the opium poppy has been in use since Neolithic times, and its virtues were known and noted in many ancient manuscripts. The Abbot of Reichenau, Walafried Strabo, the Cross-eyed, grew it in his monastery garden on

Lake Constance, among his other medicinal herbs and vegetables. Three centuries later it was still in cultivation by the monks, and Alexander Neckham, Abbot of Cirencester, mentions 'the drowsy poppy'[8] growing in his garden.

There were many ornamental poppies by the end of the seventeenth century. Here is Leonard Meager in 1699, writing of double poppies. 'These are not to be omitted though they give no fragrant scent; they are of various colours, though of one kind; some red, others purple, some white, others scarlet, and some again white-blush, others parti-colour; one Leaf half scarlet, and half white, some striped with the same colour, but those chiefly esteemed, are of a Gold yellow, double flowering and produce much seed.'[9]

Oriental poppies were introduced into this country by London and Wise.

The horned poppy has no place in the Poorman's Nosegay, and the Shirley poppy is a comparative newcomer. Bred from a sport which appeared in the garden of the Reverend Wilks in Shirley, it has given its name to a public house nearby — a rare distinction for a flower, except for the Tudor rose, and as rare a distinction for a pub.

Stock

A not very shapely beauty, with small grey-green leaves and flowers of the colours and perfume of cachou. Even its name, stock, is no name to give a flower. *Matthiola*, after the Italian physician and botanist Pierandrea Mattioli, is a little more distinguished, but the poor stock, alias *Matthiola*, has not succeeded in picking up a single affectionate country name except for gillyflower, and that it has to share with the carnation and the wallflower. The learned Dr Turner, in his history of plants calls it 'Gelour', to which he adds the word 'stock', as we would say, Gelours that grow on a stem or stock, to distinguish them from Clove Gelours and Wall Gelours.

Sir Hugh Platt, in *The Garden of Eden*, of 1653, gives the most exhaustive directions for doubling a single flower: 'Remove a plant of Stock Gilliflowers when it is a little wooded, and not too green, and water it presently. Doe this three days after the full (moon) and remove it twice more before the change. Doe this in barren ground; and likewise, three days after the next Full Moone, remove again; and then remove once more before the change. Then at the third full Moon, viz: eight days after, remove again, and set it in very rich ground, and this will make it to bring forth a double flower; but if your stock Gilliflowers once spindle, then you may not remove them.'

Leonard Meager has more practical advice on this subject in *The New Art of Gardening* of 1699 'Though some think they can make this doubling by Art, by using Insuccations, Magnomism or Medianes, yet they will find themselves mistaken, or especially it is with greater certainty done by removing, transplanting, enriching the Mould, strewing and hardening the Ground, and so for Variation and Change, taking from the Root the free Nourishment.'

Gerard says that 'they are not used in Physicke, except amongst certaine Empericks and Quacksalvers about love and lust matters, which for modestie I omit.' Less modest than Gerard, I would gladly tell you more, but I lack the information.

The Ten Weeks Stocks were developed from the Sea Stock Gillyflower discovered by John Tradescant, and grown by him in his garden at Lambeth. That this was a true Poorman's flower is proved by Jane Loudon, who says that in its finest form it was grown by the weavers of Upper Saxony, 'who take as much pleasure in growing and saving the seed of their stocks, as the Lancashire weavers do in England, in growing their pinks and carnations.'[1] It is reported that by consent, or perhaps by some municipal regulation, only one colour or variety was allowed to be grown in one village, so that the shades were kept distinct. They were sorted and packed into sets or collections, and labelled according to colour. The leaves were used for salads and potherbs.

The Brompton Stock was developed by London and Wise, the famous nurserymen whose business was founded at Brompton in 1681. They supplied the new gardens at Blenheim Palace, and so the Brompton Stock was probably grown there.

Although it is now forced, enlarged and prettified for flower arrangers, the stock, like its name, has little real beauty. It is only at night, when darkness reduces it to a pale glimmer, and its perfume waits at the window to be let in, that it has its hour of glory.

Dame's Violet or Sweet Rocket

Hesperis   Lust, vanity, rivalry, falsehood and deceit!

One cannot think why the sweet rocket should have earned for itself such a variety of unpleasant meanings. Looking through a number of worn little books, each of which claims to be the authorized version of *The Language of Flowers*, one learns never to offer as much as a single bloom to a friend, unless it is one of those friends whom you really do not like at all.

This homely and unfortunate plant is one of the Plain-Janes of the cottage garden, for even its German name of Dame's Violet has a suggestion of middle-age spread about it. German housewives loved it, and grew it in pots in their apartments. It was also known to them as Night Violet, or Night Rocket.

The rockets' homely looks by day are recompensed by their sweet night scent. As Tom Moore wrote of the jasmine, they

> Keep their odour to themselves all day
> But when the sunlight dies away
> Let the delicious secret out
> To every breeze that roams about,

and one wonders, after all, if the Dame's Violet is no better than she should be, in spite of her matronly appearance.

It seems that this scent is of short duration in individual plants, for it is said that when it was first brought to America by European settlers, it lost its scent the second season, and had to be renewed by the importation of fresh seeds from Europe.

'Sir' John Hill, in *Eden: or, a Compleat Body of Gardening*, says, 'The garden does not afford a sweeter Flower than this; though the whole Plant has much the aspect of a pretty Weed.

159

We distinguish it by the Name single (hesperis) because there is a double Species, though not known by the same Name: in that State the Plant is called Rocket; a very ill-chosen and improper term.'

'Sir' John Hill, by the way, was an interesting and probably much maligned character. Born in 1716, he became a physician, dramatist, actor, garden designer, and journalist, and was the author of many botanical works, including *The Vegetable System* and *Eden: or, a Compleat Body of Gardening*. This man of many talents was the personification of Jack-of-all-trades and Master of none, and on this account was the butt of eighteen-century wit and epigram. He was even made the subject of a mock epic, the *Hilliad*, by Christopher Smart, the onlie begetter of our title *Poorman's Nosegay*. Criticized by doctors for his practice of medicine, by botanists for his botanical works, and by playwrights for his farces, even his title was said to be spurious. David Garrick wrote,

> For physic and farces his equal there scarce is:
> His farces are physic, his physic a farce is,[1]

and the following anonymous verse is even more savage:

> Thou essence of dock, and valerian, and sage,
> At once the disgrace and the pest of your age;
> The worst that we wish thee, for all thy sad crimes,
> Is to take thine own physic, and read thine own rhymes.

Poor 'Sir' John. And yet *Eden* is an impressive book with more than fifty splendid plates, some taken from earlier botanical books and others by Van Huysum, Edwards and himself. Perhaps the laugh is with him, for it is worth a lot of money today.

According to Wilfrid Blunt, he died 'from gout, a complaint for which he professed to have discovered a sovereign remedy.'[2]

But to return to Hill's 'improper' rocket, which was introduced from Italy by Gerard in 1579.

It was one of the favourite flowers of Marie Antoinette, who loved simple flowers, and it was probably sent to her from the provinces, for it does not thrive near big cities, although easily cultivated in this country. Women used to mix it with vinegar, as a cure for freckles.

At the turn of the century, one enthusiastic gardener wrote, 'It makes one happy even to think of double rockets. They are among the most valuable of flowers for scent and pleasant association, for they are real old English things, I am convinced, though the horticultural books assign them to Southern Europe and Asia. If Shakespeare did not know them and love them I am sorry for him.'[3]

Monkshood

Aconite – the poisoner in monk's clothing – is the Rasputin of the plant world.

'Monk's-hood is very common in the Gardens remote from London, but in those near the City it is rarely found; the flowers are of a deep blue, and of a surprizing Make; they are so poisonous that I have heard the eating only six or seven of the Blossoms in a salad, has killed a Gentleman in France, who was not apprised of their evil Quality.'[1]

Henry Phillips is very nasty about it: 'We could never find sufficient beauties in these plants to justify their common cultivation in our pleasure grounds, and we shall be glad to see them entirely expelled from the gardens of the cottagers, where they are generally found in the greatest abundance. In our history of the Aconitum we shall have to relate such terrible effects of its virulent nature as must make us rejoice that it is not an indigenous plant of our soil',[2] although it has been found growing wild in woods and by the sides of streams in Devonshire, Somersetshire, Herefordshire and Gloucestershire – probably a garden escape.

John Parkinson describes the flowers as 'Of a perfect or faire blew colour, (but grow darker, having stood long) which causeth it to be so nourished up in Gardens, that their flowers, as was usuall in former times, and yet is in many Countrey places, may be laid among greene herbes in windowes and roomes for the Summer time'; but, he warns, 'although their beauty may be entertained for the uses aforesaid, yet beware they come not neare your tongue or lippes, lest they tell you to your cost, they are not so good as they seem to be.'

But Walafried Strabo, the Cross-eyed monk, who was one of

Pl. 38.

European Trollius.

The Flaming Tulip.

The Pearl & Purple Tulip.

Yellow Moly.

Alter ↑ ↑ nate flower'd Gladiolus.

Great Crimson Peony.

Fleshy late Fritillary.

PLATE 5

Trollius, Tulip, Moly, Gladiolus, Peony, Fritillary

Engraving, unsigned. From *Eden: or, a Compleat Body of Gardening,* 'Sir' John Hill, 1762.

The Capsule.

PLATE 6

Poppy

Engraving, Henderson del. Maxel sculp. (1810). From
Elements of Botany, Dr. R. J. Thornton, 1812. (One of
7000 copies issued in the Royal Botanic Lottery, under
the patronage of the Prince Regent.)

the earliest garden poets, has an instant remedy. If you fear that your stepmother may have made a treacherous dish of aconite for you, he prescribes a dose of wholesome horehound to counteract the poison.

Yet in spite of all these warnings, Thomas Fairchild in *The City Garden* in 1772, recommends monkshood as a plant that will grow very well in London.

To me, the midnight blue helmets stand in tiers like the chorus of some Wagnerian opera. Andrew Young says that it 'hides its evil nature under the mask of religion, calling itself "Monkshood",'[3] but in spite of its shady character, it answers to many innocent names, such as Grannie's Nightcap, Auld Wife's Huid, Luckie's Mutch, Friar's Cap, Chariot and Horses, (from the form of the petals when freed from their covering hood), Captain over the Garden, and the cheerful if deceptive, Dumbledore's Delight. 'Betsey called it the Dumbledore's Delight, and was not aware that the plant, in whose helmet – rather than the cowl-shaped flowers – that busy and best natured of all insects appears to revel more than in any other, is the deadly aconite.'[4]

Linnaeus says that criminals were formerly put to death with doses of aconite, and when the men of Ceos grew old and infirm they were compelled to drink of it. It was also used by Indians to poison the water in the tanks and so impede the progress of their enemies. Hunters after tigers tipped their arrows with its juice.

It was once grown on a small scale in Suffolk and Hertford-shire to supply the drug *aconiti radix*, used in fevers, and to relieve neuralgia and rheumatism.

> No, no! go not to Lethe, neither twist
> Wolf's bane, tight-rooted, for its poisonous wine.[5]

It certainly sprang from pretty unpromising beginnings. Invented by Hecate, it arose from the foam of Cerberus when Hercules dragged that unlovable beast from the regions of Pluto. No wonder that it grew up to be the problem plant of the floral world.

The united vessel of their blood,
Mingled with venom of suggestion —
As, force perforce, the age will pour it in —
Shall never leak, though it do work as strong
As Aconitum or rash gunpowder.[6]

Mignonette

Although regarded as an old-fashioned flower, mignonette was a comparative newcomer to the cottage garden, for when Napoleon was fighting in Egypt he sent mignonette seeds to Josephine to grow in her garden at Malmaison. In its native countries mignonette is a shrub, and here it may be over-wintered in the house and potted on until it becomes in two or three years a woody-stemmed bush. Josephine was the first to grow mignonette as a pot plant, and she was responsible for its popularity in France. For many years small bunches were sold in the streets of Paris.

In a manuscript note found in the library of Sir Joseph Banks, it appears that seeds, which were obtained from the Royal Gardens in Paris in 1742, were sent by Lord Bateman to his son Richard at Windsor. Ten years later Phillip Miller received seeds from Dr Adrien van Royden of Leyden, which were cultivated in the Botanic Gardens at Chelsea. From there it reached the gardens of the London florists, where it became a favourite balcony plant.

Mignonette window boxes were particularly loved by the Victorians, and Tennyson, when writing of Alice, the miller's beautiful daughter, says,

> For, you remember, you had set,
> > That morning, on the casement edge
> A long green box of mignonette.

In July, 1851, Dickens, in a letter to Lord Carlisle, suggested another use for his. 'As we think of putting mignonette boxes outside the windows for the younger children to sleep in by-and-by, I am afraid we should give your servant the cramp if we hardily undertook to lodge him.'

Mignonette was also the favourite flower of the redoubtable Mrs Beeton.

Its dusty fragrance is lessening with the years, and with it, its popularity. In 1829, Henry Phillips wrote that he considered that its scent protected Londoners from the disease brought by the stinks of the summer streets. Jean Jacques Rousseau likened it to the scent of fresh raspberries, which suggests a slight sharpness that now seems lost. The dried flowers retained their scent for several months, which is probably the reason why the ancient Egyptians used them to adorn the couches on which the mummies were laid in their tombs.

The plant is apt to grow straggly, and germination is not always satisfactory.

> Let dull instruction here remind
> That mignonette is tricky, and demands
> Firm soil, and lime, to follow your commands,
> Else failure comes, and shows a barren space
> Where you had looked for small but scented spires.[1]

To a little girl growing up on a farm in the country, mignonette developed a personality which might never have been achieved had she known it by the name of *Reseda*. 'Below in the flower-bed was Minnie Net, a sturdy little girl who carried green bags of seeds, not unlike my own gathered hanging-pocket. It was perhaps a work-bag to hold scissors and thimble for little Minnie Net. She was a person of character, with perfume in her pockets, and we took a great interest in her stay with us each summer.'[2]

Although not very handsome, because of its scent mignonette was a flower of romance, and so it seemed to Francis Kilvert, a young curate who could never resist a flower, nor a pretty face. This little love story, which might have been written, folded and sealed in one of its little green seed bags, opens in his diary on Friday, 8 September 1871: 'Perhaps this may be the most memorable day in my life.' The entry ends, after a description of a croquet party, 'Today I fell in love with Fanny (Daisy) Thomas.' And then, ten days later, 'Daisy went to her own little garden which she had when she was a child and has still and gathered from it a scarlet geranium leaf which she put into her own dress. We went down the broad middle garden walk and presently came to a large bed of mignonette which scented the whole air . . . she gathered me some mignonette, took the geranium out of her dress, and made up a nosegay which she gave to me. "It is from my own garden," she said. "I shall value it all the more," said I.'

'5 April 1872. "Talking of flowers," I said, "do you remember once last September giving me some flowers out of your own garden?" "Yes," she said, blushing prettily and looking down. "I have those flowers now," I said. "I have kept them carefully ever since, and I prize them more than I can tell you . . . I shall keep them until you give me some more".'

Kilvert had not long to wait. On 12 July 1872, is the entry: 'Daisy gave me a rose.'

But alas, a poor parish priest was not considered 'suitable' by papa. Francis Kilvert married Elizabeth Anne Rowland in 1879, and Daisy died unmarried.

Lily

One of the oldest and most beautiful flowers on earth, the lily is believed to be a survival of the Ice Age. Of its many varieties, the Madonna Lily is possibly the oldest in existence, and it is the most likely to be found in a cottage garden. Indeed, it is said that Madonna Lilies prefer the poor man to the rich.

It is the holy flower of Easter, of the Resurrection, and of the Annunciation. It is the flower of weddings and of funerals.

> Is not the Lily pure?
> What fuller can procure
> A white so perfect, spotless, clear
> As in this flower doth appear.[1]

Known until Tudor days simply as the 'lily', or the 'white lily', it was not called the Madonna Lily until the late nineteenth century, and as the 'white lily' it came to share with the rose the honour of symbolizing the Immaculate Conception. It also appears at the Feast of the Visitation, 2 July, to commemorate the journey that Mary took to visit her cousin Elizabeth. In paintings of this event there is usually a vase of three white lilies standing at the Virgin's side. This is said to have been in consequence of the three white lilies which appeared to confirm the faith of a master of the Dominican monks. Cistercian monks adopted a single flower as emblem of the Virgin in their churches.

> Last night methought I saw
> That maiden saint who stands with lily in hand
>   In yonder shrine. All round her prest the dark,
> And all the light upon her silver face
>   Flow'd from the spiritual lily that she held.[2]

Dante Gabriel Rossetti's Blessed Damozel carried three white lilies, and three symbolic lilies appear in the arms of the City of Winchester, as well as in those of the College.

> O lovely lily clean,
> O lily springing green,
> O lily bursting white,
> Dear lily of delight,
> Spring in my heart agen
> That I may flower to men.[3]

It appeared in the art of the earliest civilizations. To the Egyptians it was the emblem of fruitfulness. In ancient Greece it was the flower of Hera, the goddess of the moon. It was painted on the walls of the Cretan palace of Knossos, and found in Minoan and Assyrian art. In Rome it was the emblem of Juno, from whose milk it sprang, and so was called Juno's Rose. An old Semitic legend tells how the lily grew from the tears of Eve when she was expelled from the Garden of Eden. The pillars of Solomon's temple were topped with sculptured lily forms.

They were grown in monastery gardens both for the decoration of the church and for medicinal purposes. They were also used as pot plants for indoors. Walafried Strabo grew them in his garden in the ninth century, and used them crushed in wine as a remedy for snake bite. Centuries later, Godorus, serjeant-surgeon to Queen Elizabeth I, was said to have cured many people of dropsy, with the juice of lily roots mixed with barley flower, baked in cakes, and eaten with meat instead of other bread, for the space of a month. Most unromantically, the root of this beautiful flower was used for removing corns. There is an old recipe for a remedy for cuts and bruises which sounds like a liqueur.

Gather 'firm white lily petals while still fresh, place them unbroken in a wide-necked bottle packed closely and firmly together, and then pour in what brandy there is room for.'[4] Since it doesn't actually say that the prescription is to be applied externally, a liqueur glass full taken after dinner each evening might prove efficacious for almost anything.

Seldom have lilies been regarded as male flowers, but Maeterlinck wrote of them: 'Meanwhile, in a blaze of light, the great white Lily, the old lord of the gardens, the only authentic prince — with his invariable six-petalled chalice of silver, whose nobility dates back to that of the gods themselves — raises his ancient sceptre, august, inviolate.'[5]

Mary Webb compares the flowers to white milch kine — 'White lilies, their pale and flaking bulbs heavy with the June glories of great chalices and golden pollen, recalling in their stately promise a herd of white milch kine.'[6]

Often the flowers are likened to nuns. 'Lilies with pale faces like a procession of nuns,'[7] and that it is how they appeared to Burne-Jones and the Pre-Raphaelites.

> And this pale nun, who neither spins nor cards,
> ne cares nor frets,
> But to her mother nature all her care she lets,[8]

does she not toil like other flowers? Pushing down roots into the dark earth to brace her tall stem against the fretting winds; pushing up first the strong green leaves, and finally the sculptured buds; striving to maintain her place over the years among encroaching weeds and other and more rampant cottage flowers, is this not toil? If nature did not live a navvy's life, as Ralph Hodgson says, our gardens would be deserts in spite of all our pains.

> O silly lily
> To toil not nor to spin.
> Unless you strive to be a taller, whiter lily,
> Boredom sets in.

Rose

'What a pother have authors made with Roses! What a racket have they kept? I shall add, red Roses are under Jupiter, Damask under Venus, White under the Moon, and Provence under the King of France. . . . To write at large of every one of these, would make my book smell too big,' wrote Culpeper in his herbal.

Too well I understand how he felt, but not to write at all of this emblem of our country, this flower of love and war, of pageantry and ancient history; to search the Poorman's Nose-gay in vain for a rose, this would be unthinkable, for as Gerard says, 'the Rose doth deserve the cheefest and most principall place among all flowers whatsoever, being not onely esteemed for his beautie, vertues, and his fragrant smell, but also because it is the honore and ornament of our English Sceptre.'

The rose indeed belongs to all the world; even in the far North, where summer lasts a brief two months, the Esquimau may adorn his seal-skin coat with a posy of *Rosa nitida*, to keep up with the rose-loving Joneses of the rest of the globe.

Some say that the English dog rose was so called because it is common and without scent, like the dog violet; older writers believed that the roots contained a cure for the bite of a mad dog; and yet another theory held that the word came from 'dagge', an old English word for dagger, because of its sharp thorns. Shakespeare knew it by the name of Canker rose, and that name survived with the roses in the Devonshire lanes for more than three hundred years.

Rosamund de Clifford, Henry II's Fair Rosamund, brought wild roses from the wood and planted them in the secret garden that Henry had made for her.

ROSAMUND: There is a bench. Come wilt thou sit?
My bank of wild flowers
(He sits.) At thy feet! (She sits at his feet.)
HENRY II: I bade them clear
A royal pleasaunce for thee, in the wood,
Not leave these countryfolk at court.
ROSAMUND: I brought them
In from the wood, and set them here, I love them
More than the garden flowers, that seem at most
Sweet guests, or foreign cousins, not half speaking
The language of the land. I love them too,
Yes. But, my liege, I am sure, of all the roses –
Shame fall on those who give it a dog's name –
This wild rose – nay, I shall not prick myself –
Is sweetest.[1]

But when the single rose was brought in from the wild into Far Eastern gardens, golden stamens began to develop into petals, and gradually the double, scented, rose was born.

The wild rose in a sheltered garden
when it need struggle no more
softly blows out its thin little male stamens
into broad sweet petals,
and through the centuries goes on and on
puffing its little male stamens out into sterile petal flames
till at last it's a full, full rose, and has no male dust any more,
it propagates no more,[2]

and its future lies in budding and grafting and layering, and the skilful hands of the nurseryman.

With the perfume of the double roses came trade, and in Alexandria, Tunis, Constantinople and many parts of Persia roses were grown for the making of perfume. Not more than one ounce of attar could be made from three hundred pounds of petals, and so it was a common sight to see petals piled into stacks like haystacks, ready to be taken away for distilling. There is a traveller's tale of a breakfast given to Sir John

172

Malcolm, our envoy to the court of Persia, which was celebrated on top of one of these stacks of roses. Another story
tells of a courier bringing despatches overland from Constantinople to the British Government, who was waylayed
and robbed of everything he carried. Among his luggage were
several bottles of attar of roses, one of which was broken in the
struggle. The perfume was so strong that it guided the officers
of justice to the thieves' hideout. Hermetically sealed phials
containing attar of roses were found in the tomb of an Egyptian
princess.

The bed of roses was not only a metaphor for a life of luxury.
Roses grew in the garden of the Nile, and from their petals
mattresses were made for people of rank to lie on. Amongst the
Greeks also, there was an old joke told against the effeminate
Sybarites, that when one of them complained that he had not
slept all night, the reason he gave was that one of the petals
in his mattress had become folded under him, an ancient version of *The Princess and the Pea.*

Roman emperors who wished to honour their victorious
generals, allowed them to add a rose to the ornament on their
shields, a custom which lasted long after the fall of the Roman
Empire, and which may yet be traced in the armorial bearings
of many of the ancient noble families of Europe. Roses were also
planted on Roman graves, a custom they brought with them
during their occupation.

It seems that at all times, in people's hearts came

> First of all the rose, because its breath
> Is rich beyond the rest, and when it dies
> It doth bequeath a charm to sweeten death.[3]

Wreaths and garlands of roses were worn at Greek festivals,
and the very irreverent Dean Hole, Dean of Rochester, found
himself 'wondering whether the nimble earwig ever ran down
their Grecian noses,' a very real danger, it would seem, when
one studies the classic profile and observes the direct run
offered to an insect who wished to make a hasty getaway.

But to our own garden roses. 'Will you accompany me, my

reader, to one of Queen Rosa's levees? They differ in some points from Queen Victoria's — as, for example, in these: that the best time to attend them is at sunrise; that you may go to them with dressing-gown and slippers, or with shooting-coat and short pipe; that the whole court will smile upon you according to your loyalty, not according to your looks or your income; and that all the beauty which you see will be real — no false foliage, no somebody-else's ringlets, no rouge, no pastes, no powders, no perfumes but their own.

'Enter, then, the Rose-garden when the first sunshine sparkles in the dew, and enjoy with thankful happiness one of the loveliest scenes of earth. . . . There are White Roses, Striped Roses, Blush Roses, Pink Roses, Rose Roses, Carmine Roses, Crimson Roses, Scarlet Roses, Vermilion Roses, Maroon Roses, Purple Roses, Roses almost Black and Roses of a glowing Gold.'[4] And, one might add today, Lilac and so-called Blue.

Dean Hole was the first President of the National Rose Society nearly a century ago, and when, at as far distant a date as possible, I hope, Harry Wheatcroft arrives in heaven, I think the old Dean will be waiting eagerly to discuss the latest development in rose breeding. No time to talk of cabbages and kings, unless they be Cabbage Roses and King's Ransom; but 'Dwarf Roses and climbing Roses, Roses closely carpeting the ground, Roses that droop in snowy foam like fountains, and Roses that stretch out their branches upwards as though they would kiss the sun; Roses "in shape no bigger than an agate-stone on the forefinger of an alderman," and Roses five inches across; Roses in clusters, and Roses blooming singly; Roses in bud, in their glory, decline, and fall.'[4] So much did he love his roses, it is said, that the Dean had to leave home at pruning time, because he couldn't bear to see it done. To him it must have seemed like watching his children having their tonsils out.

But John Wilkes, whose stormy political career, one would have thought, left little time for roses, was made of sterner stuff. In a letter to his daughter he wrote, 'I cut off all the rose-buds of the trees in our little garden (which is a secret) to make them blow at the end of the season, when I hope to enjoy your company there.'[5]

If one had to choose only one type of rose — Shrub Rose, China Rose, Alba, Damask, Moss — which would it be? Scent is perhaps of the first importance, and after that, the longest blooming period; so that one can cram more roses and more perfume into the short weeks of summer.

'If anything could make me wish to have a large house instead of a small one, it would be that I might have a wider expanse of wall up which to grow clambering roses. For from being surprised that there was once a War of the Roses, I wonder the world is not perpetually at war about them, there are so many claimants for the crown. . . . Sometimes I think that I should like nothing but tea-roses; but the fit of unreasonable exclusiveness soon passes away.'[6]

> You love the Roses — so do I. I wish
> The sky would rain down Roses, as they rain
> From off the shaken bush. Why will it not?
> Then all the valley would be pink and white
> And soft to tread on. They would fall as light
> As feathers, smelling sweet; and it would be
> Like sleeping and like waking, all at once.[7]

The Red Rose

After the 'raptures and roses of vice' in Rome, the wearing of garlands was out of favour until the early Christians made the red rose the symbol of the martyr's blood, and garlands of red roses were laid on their sepulchres in the catacombs.

In Turkey the red rose was believed to be coloured with the blood of Mohammed, and the petals were never allowed to lie on the ground.

'The miserably infatuated Turkes will not suffer a Rose leafe to lye upon the ground or any to tread on them in honour of their Mahomet, from whose Sweat they are persuaded the Rose sprang up; somewhat like unto the old Pagans who held the Rose which formerly was white to become red from the blood of Venus, falling thereon from her foote hurt by a thorne, as she ran among the bushes to help her Adonis,' thus wrote our kindly Parkinson, for once intolerant.

The rose being now a Christian emblem, it was worn by medieval priests in garlands and chaplets on church festivals until the Reformation. Red roses were strung together by St Dominic, each one a symbol of prayer, and thus the first rosary was made; and because rose petals were afterwards pressed into moulds to make beads and threaded together, they were called a rosary. During Our Lady's month of May in Italy, roses are present everywhere as a symbol of the Virgin.

In the Middle Ages, the idea of the red rose was connected with the idea of blood, and it was believed that if you spilt a drop of your own blood under a rose bush, it would give you ruddy cheeks. It was also considered a remedy for haemorrhage.

The annual rendering of a red rose is one of the commonest kinds of quit-rent mentioned in old conveyances. Sir Christopher Hatton held his estate, Hatton Garden, on a tenure of a red rose at Midsummer and ten loads of hay; and on the

estate of Overponds, near Shakleford in Surrey, there was until
some forty years ago, a cottage held on lease for a thousand
years from the thirty-first year of Queen Elizabeth's reign, at
the yearly rent of one red rose.

Today the old beliefs are dropping away like fallen petals,
yet still

> Roses are beauty, but I never see
> Those blood drops from the burning heart of June
> Glowing like thought upon the living tree
> Without a pity that they die so soon.[1]

The White Rose

The white rose has played many parts in history, and as a title it has been bestowed on both men and women. In 1455, when the most bloody battles in English history tore England apart, the white rose became the symbol of the House of York. In the quiet of the Temple Garden the quarrel between the dukes of York and Lancaster began, when Warwick sided with Plantagenet. 'I love no colours, and without all colour Of base insinuating flattery I pluck this white rose with Plantagenet'; and Vernon with Warwick, 'Then for the truth and plainness of the case, I pluck this pale and maiden blossom here, Giving my verdict on the white rose side.'[1]

This pale emblem was worn throughout the thirty years of civil war, until red and white were united by the marriage of Henry Tudor with Elizabeth Plantagenet, and the red and white Tudor rose was born. T. S. Eliot always wore a white rose on the anniversary of the Battle of Bosworth, where Richard III was slain, because, he insisted, Richard III was the last true English king.

The title of the White Rose was bestowed on more than one Yorkist adherent. The mother of Edward IV, Cecily Nevill, was known as the White Rose of Raby; but Edward's sister, Margaret of Burgundy, transferred the title of the White Rose of England to Perkin Warbeck, the Pretender, who claimed to be the son of Edward IV, but was executed in 1499. His wife, Lady Catharine Gordon, was also called the White Rose, so easily were titles given and transferred.

Edward IV was born in Rouen in 1441, and called the Rose of Rouen. He claimed the English throne when he was nineteen. Here are lines from his coronation song:

> There sprung a Rose in Rouen grown to great honour;
> Had not the Rose of Rouen been, all England had been dour;
> Y-blessed be the time God ever spread that flower.

PLATE 7

Rosemary and Violet

Hand-coloured engraving by William Clark, engraver to
the London Horticultural Society, from *The Moral of
Flowers*, Mrs. Hey, 1835.

PLATE 8

Roses, Sunflower, Carnations, Poppies

Engraving, J. Hill del. et sculp. From *Eden: or, a Compleat Body of Gardening*, 'Sir' John Hill, 1762.

He fought at the Battle of Mortimer Cross, where the sun appeared to him like three suns suddenly joined into one, a phenomenon which it was believed actually occurred at that time.

> Three suns were seen that instant to appear
> Which soon againe shut up themselves in one.
> So that thereby encouraging his men
> Once more he sets the White Rose up again,

and this same White Rose *en Soleil* appeared in his arms to celebrate his victory.

That the existence of a rose tree bearing both red and white roses before the outcome of the Civil Wars had been rumoured is mentioned by Parkinson, although he seems not altogether convinced. 'It is too lamentably knowne in this Land, the civill warres betweene the houses of the two brethren John of Gaunt Duke of Lancaster, and Edmond of Langley Duke of Yorke the one making a red Rose his cognisance for them and their followers, and the other a white: but it is sayd that before this division there was seene at Longleete a White Rose tree to beare on the oneside faire white Roses, and on the other side red, prognosticating as it were both these families, which may be as true as that a white Hen with a sprigge of bayes in the mouth, lighted into the lappe of Livia Augusta.'

This same white rose became the Jacobite rose, and 10 June was called White Rose Day, in celebration of the birth of the Old Pretender, as James Francis Edward, son of James II was called.

> Of all the days that's in the year,
> The tenth of June I love most dear,
> When sweet white roses do appear,
> For the sake of James the rover![2]

James's son, Charles Edward, the Young Pretender, Bonny Prince Charlie to his adherents, took over the white rose and it flourished in many a Scottish garden, and spoke of loyalty to the Jacobite cause in silence more pregnant than words. 'On the shady side of the garden, among the potatoes, distinguished by its grace of growth, by its bluish green leaf, and its half single snow-white flower, we know the ancient Jacobite rose. Until I knew its name, it used to seem so strange, that in some parts, never a road-side cottage, or little muirland dwelling, if no more than a "butt and ben", but had its white rose growing by the door, or straggling across the dyke. It is the old Jacobite rose, and its presence thus surviving among us still, is a living link with those far-off troubled times, when Prince Charles was the darling of the people, and his rose, "the rose that's like the snaw", was planted by every house wall in that north land of loyalty. They had their white rose always near, though they might not dare to wear it.'[3]

> The green leaf o' loyalty's beginning now to fa',
> The bonnie White Rose it is withering an' a';
> But we'll water it with the blude o' usurping tyrannie,
> An' fresh it shall blaw in my ain countrie,

And fresh it was still growing in the garden of Huntercombe Manor in 1859, 'a gift straight from a garden in the Canonry, Aberdeen Old Town, where it has "always been", as one says. It is the very rose they loved and wore for Prince Charlie.'[3]

The white rose is generally connected with death in folklore. In Scotland it was planted on the graves of children, and in Wales on the graves of the young and unmarried. In Germany, if a white rose bloomed in late autumn it was said to forecast the death of a member of the household; but if the petals of a white rose fall on you, your Angel is praying for you.

> Where shall I find a white rose blowing?
> Out in the garden where all sweets be.
> But out in my garden the snow was snowing
> And never a white rose opened for me.[4]

The juice of the petals produced a yellow colouring matter. 'The white leaves stamped in a wooden dish with a piece of Allum and the juyce strained forth into some glased vessell, dried in the shadow, and kept, is the most fine and pleasant yellow colour that may be divised, not onely to limne or wash pictures and Imagerie in books, but also to colour meats and sauces, which notwithstanding the Allum is very wholesome.'[5]

In spite of a blood-stained past, there is cool perfection in the half-opened bud of a white rose.

> White roses set in ivory urns,
>   White violets wreathed in silver cups;
> White marble founts whose moss and ferns
>   The shadow of the moon drink up.[6]

The Briar Rose

The green leaves of the sweet briar were commonly used in France to flavour liqueurs, but in England, in sober contrast, a sweet briar tea was made and taken as a tonic. The ends of the shoots were sometimes candied as a dessert, and up to the beginning of this century conserve of roses was still to be had from druggists' shops, just as it was in the apothecary's store in *Romeo and Juliet*.

> About his shelves
> A beggarly account of empty boxes,
> Green earthen pots, bladders, and musty seeds,
> Remnants of packthreads and old cakes of roses.[1]

My mother used to tell me of the bladders of lard which were scented with roses by her grandfather, and made up into jars which her grandmother sold in their little bow-fronted herbalist's shop in Ben Jonson Road in the City. This beautifying face cream, the old herbalist said with his gentle smile, couldn't possibly do the young ladies any harm, even if it didn't actually do them any good.

Rosebuds were sometimes pickled in vinegar, or preserved in sugar, and offered as birthday gifts. In the reign of Queen Elizabeth I the wild briar hips were made by cooks and gentlewomen into tarts and conserve, and in the reign of the second Queen Elizabeth babies are still brought up on rose hip syrup.

William Beckford spoke of the use of rose petals in the bath. 'You know how warmly every mortal of taste delights in these lovely flowers. . . . Has not Lady —— a whole apartment painted over with roses? Does she not fill her bath with their leaves, and deck her idols with garlands of no other flowers? and is she not quite in the right of it?'[2]

Sweet briar still grows in cottage gardens, and surely there is nothing more earthily fragrant than its dripping leaves after a shower? It used to be cut from the country lanes and hawked about the streets of London, together with branches of May; ten shillings' worth in a full hamper, sold in pennyworths. Here are sweet briars in a pleasant Edwardian picture: 'Two tall sweet briers guard the entrance of the brier cross-walk. Today they are covered with little pink roses, like nothing I have ever seen since Masaccio's fresco in the Ricardi palace at Florence, where rose-crowned angels kneel in a row beside a low rose hedge.'[3]

It was the wild rose that brought back memories of a childish rose-wreathed straw hat to Mrs Hey, a lady who in 1836 published *The Moral of Flowers*, a book of period charm that is now a collector's piece, for its hand-coloured plates if not for its sentimental verses.

> Yes! gazing on thee now,
> Those scenes beloved can memory draw
> When simple childhood's hat of straw
>   Shaded my careless brow:
> And round it cluster'd many a wreath
>   Of blossoms wild and sweet as thou,
> And lighter was the heart beneath
>   Than it is now.

I can see that hat.

Rosemary

This ancient plant, a part of English history, came originally from the Mediterranean coasts, where it was known as Rosmarine, the bush of the sea-spray; a floral Venus rising from the foam. It was also called Libanotis, from its smelling like incense, and Coronarius, because women made crowns and garlands of it. John Evelyn mentions among other fragrant shrubs, 'rosemary, the flowers of which are credibly reported to give their scent about thirty leagues off at sea upon the coasts of Spain.'[1] It is thought to have been brought to England by the Romans.

Its name is forever linked with that of Sir Thomas More and Chelsea in the sixteenth century, when Chelsea was a country village. 'As for Rosemarie I lette it run alle over my Garden Walls, not onlie because my bees love it, but because 'tis the Herb sacred to Remembrance, therefore to Friendship; whence a sprig of it hath a dumb language.'[2]

Here is a description from Lyte's *Herball* of 1578. 'Rosemary is, as it were, a little tree or wooddish shrubbe, with many small branches and slender boughes, of hard or wooddie substance, covered and set full of little, smal, long, and tender leaves, white on the side next the ground, and greene above. The floures are whitishe, and mixte with a little blewe, the which past there cometh forth small seede. The roote and the stemme are likewise hard and woodie. The leaves and the floures are of a very strong and pleasant flavour, and good smacke or taste. The oyle of the floures of Rosemary helpeth the memory.'

It was perhaps the most useful shrub in the Tudor garden. Clipped in neat outlines to the knot garden, it was also the cook's favourite garnish for lamb, chicken and pork. It was a good bee plant, and added a characteristic flavour to the honey. It was used in the ale-house for dipping in tankards and for stirring the cups at christenings and weddings; and in the apothecary's shop as a cure for hangovers, or 'the affections of the head caused by wine.' Culpeper prescribed 'the dried leaves shred small, and taken in a pipe, as tobacco is taken, for those that have cough, phthisic or consumption.'

It was standard remedy for the plague, and Thomas Decker in *The Wonderful Year 1603* remarked that the plague had been so bad that rosemary which had been wont to be sold for twelve pence an armful went now at six shillings a handful. For the same prophylactic reasons it was present in the dock of the accused in courts of justice.

It was indispensable for marriage and death ceremonies too.

> Grow for two ends: it matters not at all,
> Be't for my bridall or my buriall.[3]

It was worn by bride and groom and wedding guests alike, and 'carried in a fair bride-cup of silver-gilt . . . wherein was a goodly brand of Rosemary, gilded very fair, and hung about with silken ribbons of all colours.'[4] Anne of Cleeves, when she arrived at Greenwich as a bride, wore on her head a coronet of gold and precious stones, set full of branches of rosemary. The sprigs were dipped in scented water for weddings and plain water for funerals. At most funerals a servant presented sprays of rosemary to each guest at the nailing of the coffin. The sprigs were then thrown into the open grave.

Prue Sarn, in *Precious Bane*, describes the scene at the funeral of her father. 'Gideon behind the coffin by himself, then Mother and me in our black poke bonnets and shawls, with Prayer books and branches of rosemary in our hands.'[5] Even for the normal Sunday church going, it was carried by country-folk, for, 'Where be your sprigs of rosemary and your clean handkerchers?' says mother to Gideon and Prue, in the same book.

The Reverend Hilderic Friend has a most irreverent story of a man who wanted to marry again on the day of his wife's funeral, so that the same rosemary could be used at both ceremonies. Even grimmer is his tale of the funeral of a soldier, shot for mutiny in 1649. The corpse was adorned with bundles of rosemary, one half of each being stained with blood.

The decking of the church at Christmas was not always appreciated, however. Richard Steele, under the pseudonym of 'Jenny Simper', wrote to the *Spectator* on 14 January 1712: 'I am a young woman and have my fortune to make, for which reason I come constantly to church to hear divine service, and to make conquests: but one great hindrance in this my design, is that our clerk, who was once a gardener, has this Christmas so overdeckt the church with greens, that he has quite spoilt my prospect, insomuch that I have scarce seen the young baronet I dress at these three weeks, though we have both been very constant at our devotions, and do not sit above three pews off. The church, as it is now equipt, looks more like a green-house than a place of worship. The middle isle is a very pretty shady walk, and the pews look like so many arbours on each side of it. The pulpit itself has such clusters of ivy, holly, and rosemary about it, that a light fellow in our pew took occasion to say, that the congregation heard the word out of a bush, like Moses.'

Ten days later, Steele replied to himself, in the person of the clerk, Francis Sternhold. 'I must beg of you to publish this as a public admonition to the aforesaid Mrs. Simper, otherwise all my honest care in the disposition of the greens in the church will have no effect: I shall therefore with your leave lay before you the whole matter. I was formerly, as she charges me, for several years a gardener in the county of Kent: but I must absolutely deny, that it is out of any affection I retain for my old employment that I have placed my greens so illiberally about the church, but out of a particular spleen I conceived against Mrs. Simper (and others of the same sisterhood) some time ago. As to herself, I had one day set the hundredth Psalm, and was singing the first line in order to put the congregation into the tune, she was all the while curtsying to

Sir Anthony, in so affected and indecent a manner, that the indignation I conceived at it made me forget myself so far, as from the tune of that Psalm to wander into Southwell tune, and from thence into Windsor tune, still unable to recover myself, until I had with the utmost confusion set a new one ... I had several projects in my head to put a stop to this growing mischief; but as I have long lived in Kent, and there often heard how the Kentish men evaded the conqueror, by carrying green boughs over their heads, it put me in mind of practising this device against Mrs. Simper. I find I have preserved many a young man from her eye-shot by this means: therefore humbly pray the boughs may be fixed, until she shall give security for her peaceable intentions.'

At one time this indispensable plant was called Guard-robe, because it was 'put into chests and presses among clothes to preserve them from moths and other vermin.'[6] It gave off more an incense than a perfume. 'Make thee a box of rosemary and smell it and it shall preserve thy youth.'[6] The singing of love songs to an accompaniment on a perfumed instrument must have won the heart of many a fair Elizabethan lady, for the wood was made into 'lutes, or such like instruments,' and small tools and what we would now call 'treen' were also made.

In her diary for 24 April 1617, Anne, Countess of Dorset, notes, between entries on the new puppies, her work on her Irish stitch cushion and her frequent quarrels with her husband, 'We made Rosemary Cakes.'

To end on yet another culinary note, here is part of a letter from the poet Gray to his friend, Mr Wharton, a fellow of Pembroke College, Cambridge. '27 Dec. 1742. I was going to tell you how sorry I am for your illness, but, I hope, it is too late to be sorry now; I can only say that I really was very sorry. May you live a hundred Christmases, and eat as many collars of brawn stuck with rosemary.'

Lavender

Lavender, the grey lady of the garden, seeming to have been born and bred in an English vicarage, was brought a stranger from the sunny Mediterranean shores some time before the middle of the thirteenth century. Here she settled like a native, responding to our cloudier and moister climate, and developing over the years an English strain that is the finest in the world today.

First grown in the physic garden, lavender was mentioned by William Turner, botanist and physician to the Protector Somerset. Turner, who compiled one of the earliest English herbals, recommended that the flowers 'should be quilted in a cappe and dayle worne for all diseases of the head that come of a cold cause, and comfort the braine very well.'[1] Culpeper, in his herbal, says that 'the floures of lavender alone, or with Cinnamone, Nutmegs, and Cloves do cure the beating of the harte.'

Lavender should be chosen as the emblem of good housewifery, for women made use of it as a protection against moths, and 'for to perfume linnen, apparrell, gloves, leather, etc.,'[2] a custom handed down from mother to daughter in English homes to this day. 'To lay in lavender' might also mean 'to pawn', for pawned clothes used to be strewn with lavender to keep them fresh. It was also used to sweeten baths, and the very name, which suggests *lavare* – to wash – speaks of cleanliness. At one time it was used in every laundry, and court ruffles were scented with it in the seventeenth century. Cushions, too, were stuffed with it, and hung over the backs of chairs.

It was not only women who enjoyed the sweet scent of lavender.

'Good master, let's go to that house, for the linen looks white, and smells of lavender, and I love to lie in a pair of sheets that smell so,' wrote Izaak Walton in 1682.[3]

'Alas, no village inn can boast of its lavender-scented bed-linen as in the coaching days now far off. The broad-oak stair-cases and bright polished furniture, the cosy carven settles and the rare old china beau-pots filled as the seasons came round with snowdrops, or lilies-of-the-valley, with damask roses, or, daintier far, white roses of Provence – all these, and lavender bushes amongst them – which used to be the pride of count-less old-fashioned hostelries, where are they?'[4]

Many people remember the drying flower heads laid out in trays, with the house full of the sweetness, and the bees outside humming angrily at being deprived of so promising a source of honey. Country towns like Mitcham, as it was then, and Hitchen, and large areas of Norfolk, Suffolk, Lincolnshire, Cambridgeshire and Kent, where lavender was grown for the making of perfume, must have been pleasant places to live in.

An acre of lavender produces between ten and twenty pounds of oil; a ton of flowers, ten pounds of oil. A planted field stands for three or four years, and is then rested before re-planting. The oil is used for medicines, soap, shaving soaps and lotions, and in eau-de-Cologne and lavender water. Some var-ieties yielded an oil that was used by artists for varnishing.

As children we used to delight in making giant lavender heads. A small bunch was tied immediately beneath the flowers; the stalks were then bent back over the flowers and tied again, making a 'head', and a narrow lavender ribbon was threaded in and out of the stalks, and tied in a bow beneath the 'head'. An enchanting object, very suitable for grandma's birthday.

Lavender was an Elizabethan lover's flower. In *A Nosegaie Alwaies Sweet, for Lovers to send for tokens of love, at New Yere's Tide, or For Fairings as They in Their Minds Shall be Disposed to Write*, of 1584, it says,

Lavender is for lovers true,
Which evermore be fain,
Desiring always for to have
Some pleasure for their pain.
And when that they obtained have
The love that they require,
Then have they all their perfect joy
And quenched is the fire.[5]

And in Drayton's 'Pastorals' we find

He from his lass him lavender hath sent,
Showing her love, and doth requital crave.[6]

There is no better hedge to border a cottage garden. Neat and grey at all times of the year, and in the flowering season looking like long silvery pincushions stuck with Edwardian hat-pins. These are the flowers that memories are made of.

Periwinkle

Vinca   Sweet remembrances

Just why this oldest of old flowers, Chaucer's Pervenche, the
Little Laurel, should share the name of an ancient mollusc,
when neither bears the remotest resemblance to the other, is a
mystery. In Gloucestershire it was sometimes called Cockles,
because, since one shellfish is as good as another, the names
became interchangeable.

There are two native species, *V. major* and *V. minor*. Since
the name sounds like *vincio*, to bind, it was thought that it
may have been derived from the Latin verb. Because of this
quality, Culpeper accepts Albertus Magnus's belief that 'the
leaves of periwinkle eaten by man and wife together, cause
love together'.

The periwinkle was probably introduced by the Romans,
who wore it in wreaths on ceremonial occasions. It was used for
wreaths in many countries, and young girls wore it both in life
and death. For this reason the Italians called it Death's flower,
and country folk in England knew it as the Violet of the Dead.
In France it was considered a magic plant, and was called
Sorcerer's Violet. In the Middle Ages criminals went to their
death gruesomely wreathed in it. One of these unfortunates
was Simon Fraser, who was crowned with periwinkle as he
rode to his death on the scaffold. He was the eldest son of the
Simon Fraser who fought by the side of Sir William Wallace.
When captured, 'he was carried to London heavily ironed,
with his legs tied under his horse's belly, and as he passed
through the city a garland of Periwinkle was in mockery
placed on his head.'[1]

By the beginning of the eighteenth century white, red, blue,
purple, double and even striped periwinkles were known, many
of which have since disappeared. A red periwinkle, planted out-

191

side the garden gate, is an invitation to passers-by to come and see your garden, if only one knows how to read the signs aright. Nowadays vincas are coming into favour once more, and the dwarf forms make excellent pot- or house-plants, with their shining green leaves and their blush-pink, rose or white flowers with a neat red eye. There are also varieties with silver and gold variegated leaves, and a double plum-purple, *V. minor*, called simplex.

Beverley Nichols thinks highly of the periwinkle as ground cover, and suggests that we all become periwinklists without delay.

An ointment was prepared from vinca leaves and used by housewives for soothing skin complaints, and yet its juice is so acrid and astringent that it has been used in tanning. Long bands of the green leaves were bound about the limbs to prevent cramp. This versatile plant was known to Elizabethans as Joy of the Ground.

In Dorset I have seen woods so thickly carpeted with periwinkle that any other flower would seem an interloper in that dim green world; a world silent and still as the bottom of some deep pool. Mary Webb wrote of this stillness, 'Watch a bank of periwinkle on an early summer morning. The fresh blue flowers are poised high on delicate stalks, and seem aloof from the leaves. Absolute stillness broods over them; no tremor is discernible in leaf or petal; the wide blue flowers gaze up intently into the wide blue sky. Suddenly, without any breath of wind, without so much stir as a passing gnat makes, one flower has left her stem. No decay touched her; it was just that in her gentle progressive existence the time for erect receiving was over. Some faint vibration told her that the moment had come for her to leave off gazing stilly at the sky: and so, in silence and beauty, with soft precipitation, she buried her face in the enfolding evergreen leaves. This pale shadow of a gesture is as lovely, as inevitable, as the flight of wild swans beating up the sky.'[2]

Its meaning, sweet remembrance, was given to it by the French, because Rousseau wrote of seeing the flowers again after thirty years, and remembering a walk with Madame Warens, when they noticed its blue in a hedge, that same little flower that in Devonshire has the nice name of Blue Buttons.

Canon Ellacombe, writing of the white flower, says, 'I never saw the beautiful small white periwinkle (an uncommon plant anywhere, and even doubtfully native) so luxuriant as I once saw it on the walls of Tintern Abbey. As it grew there I could easily fancy that it was an escape from, and perhaps the last remnant of, the old Abbey garden, and for the first time I realized how well adapted the plant was to form the "garlands of Pervenke set on his head" that Chaucer and other old writers sing of; but the plant is no longer there, having been destroyed, by a succession of admiring and greedy visitors.'[3]

Fuchsia

Many years ago I was told about an Edwardian wedding in
which two auburn-haired sisters married two handsome
brothers in a double ceremony. The brides wore dresses of
fuchsia colours, violet and magenta, and so vivid was the
picture in my mind's eye, that ever since, fuchsias have meant
to me Edwardian brides in Kensington weddings wearing
striking garments of purple and salmon, heliotrope and cherry,
with an occasional lapse into the more conventional white
satin and guipure of Flying Cloud or Ting-a-Ling.

Fuchsias belong rather to the cottage window, the window-
box and the brimming hanging basket, than to the garden, and
indeed, it may have been a cottage window that saw the introduction of the first fuchsia to this country; for there is a story
that James Lee, who in 1745 started a nursery called the
Vineyard on the present site of Olympia, saw a plant on the
window-sill of a sailor's house in Wapping. The sailor's wife
was at first reluctant to sell the plant, but Lee offered her all
the money in his pockets, about eight guineas, with the
promise of the first of the young plants that he would raise
from it. She at last agreed, and Lee kept his word. It must have
been a large and healthy plant, for by next flowering season,
Lee had produced three hundred plants which he sold for a
guinea apiece.

The first fuchsia to be illustrated and described in 1703, was
by Father Plumier, a missionary botanist, who became King's
Botanist to Louis XIV. Plumier first recorded finding it in
1643, and he called it fuchsia in memory of Leonard Fuchs, a
German botanist of the sixteenth century. Fuchs was a prac-
titioner and teacher of medicine, renowned for his treatment
of an epidemic of plague in Anspach in 1529.

FUCHSIA

The plant is a native of South America, where bushes can grow to the height of a man, completely laden and dripping with flowers. A Captain Firth brought home a plant from San Domingo, which he presented to Kew in 1788. Up to the year 1823 there were only two kinds grown in this country, *F. coccinea* and *F. lycicides*, yet by the 1880s there were some fifteen hundred named sorts. But their popularity waned. By 1895 Henry Ellacombe was writing, 'A few years ago it was considered bad taste to admire a fuchsia; but I always valued them as very bright objects in the autumn gardens, and I am told that they are again becoming fashionable.'[1] In spite of this, after the First World War many varieties had been lost, but interest has revived again, as it has done with many other cottage flowers.

It has become naturalized in the hedgerows of Ireland and the West Country, especially in Devonshire where it was known as Our Lady's Eardrops. This name was taken to America with the emigrants, and there the name clung for many years.

Here is a description of the last autumn of Hazel Woodus's short life, taken from *Gone to Earth*. 'Morning by morning Hazel watched the fuchsia bushes, set with small red flowers, purple-cupped, with crimson stamens, sway in beautiful abandon. The great black bees pulled at them like a calf at its mother. Their weight dragged the slender drooping branches almost to the earth – and then one morning all was over; one of Undern's hard early frosts took them all – the waxen red-pointed buds, the waxen purple cups, the red-veined leaves.'[2]

And Thomas Hardy has a wry, dry and typical little verse.

Mrs. Masters's fuchsias hung
Higher and broader, and brightly swung,
    Bell-like, more and more
Over the narrow garden-path,
Giving the passer-by a sprinkle-bath
    In the morning.

She put up with their pushful ways,
And made us tenderly lift their sprays,
    Going to her door:
But when her funeral had to pass
They cut back all the flowery mass
    In the morning.

Sunflower

Helianthus   Haughtiness and false riches

This is a flower of dual personality. In the cottage garden it turns a bland nursery-rhyme countenance to the sun, open and upright. Cut it, bring it indoors and stand it in a vase, for you cannot 'arrange' it, and it assumes a sinister dark Inca mask, with brazen encircling hair.

It is not only artists such as Van Gogh that have given the sunflower its exotic character, for it was used in the religious ceremonies of the Incas, who worshipped the god of day. Virgins who officiated in the Temple of the Sun were crowned with sunflowers made of pure gold, carrying others in their hands and on their breasts. When the Spaniards, led by Pizarro, conquered Peru in 1532, they were dazzled by the light reflected by these golden discs, and still more astonished when they found the fields covered with the giant living flowers.

The sunflower provided sacred food for the North American Indians of the prairie regions. They placed ceremonial bowls of sunflower seeds on the graves of their dead, to sustain them on their journey to the Happy Hunting Grounds.

By 1596 it was known to Gerard by several names; the Flower of the Sunne, the Marigolde of Peru, the Indian Sun and the Golden Floure of Peru. He describes them as being 'beset around with a pale or border of goodly yellow leaves – the middle part whereof is made as it were of cloath wrought with the needle – We have found by triall, that the buds before they be floured boiled and eaten with butter, vinegar, and pepper, after the manner of Artichokes, are exceedingly pleasant meat.'

Gerard grew them in his garden in Holborn, where they grew fourteen feet high.

In Hill's *Eden* it says that 'its Seeds were some of the first which Europe received from that Quarter [Peru] and those who raised them earliest, must have been astonished as well as charmed to see the vast Stalk rise, and the enormous Flower expand its golden Petals.'

It was believed that the flower turned its head towards the sun, so that the French called it *tournesol* or *grand soleil*.

There is a legend of Clytie, a water nymph, who, saddened by the falseness of her lover Apollo, pined away and was changed into a sunflower. It seems a peculiarly tough and healthy flower to pine away into; perhaps she chose one of the smaller varieties or she would have gained little sympathy.

It became a favourite flower, almost a symbol, of Art Nouveau. Artists looked at it with fresh eyes, and outlined its tapered leaves and coarse stems with flowing, bold lines in metal, wood, textiles and pottery. 'There was a time,' says E.V.B., a garden writer of this period, 'when I did n Sunflowers. Their constant repetition as a kind of aesthetic badge can scarcely fail to tire. But once I found a little song of William Blake's:

> Ah, Sunflower! weary of time,
> Who countest the steps of the sun,

and ever since, for the music of it, the Sunflower has been beloved with the feeling that to know her is to give her your heart.'[1]

Oil, which resembles linseed oil in its properties and uses, is extracted from the seed, and for this purpose it has been cultivated in Russia, East Africa, Australia, China, America and, on a limited scale, in England.

Of recent years, three quarters of the hashish fields of the Lebanon have been turned over to the cultivation of sunflowers for oil and cattle food. After extraction, the oil cake that remains may be fed to sheep, pigs, poultry, pigeons and rabbits. The leaves can be used for fodder, the stalks burnt for fuel, and the ash which is rich in potash, returned to the land. The seeds may also be ground into meal and made into cakes, or roasted and used as coffee. It is an excellent bee flower, from which large quantities of honey and wax are obtained. In Russia the seeds are eaten as nuts, and are sold in the streets in machines, like peanuts.

Because of its vital uses to the early pioneers, it became the State flower of Kansas; and in the military cemeteries of Poland, a sunflower grows on every grave. Truly an international flower, which in its season plays many parts.

Chrysanthemum

Chrysanthemum	Cheerfulness under adversity

The chrysanthemum is a stranger and a comparative new-comer within our garden gates, but because of its value to us in the autumn, it is admitted to the Poorman's Nosegay; but only, and I am firm about this, only if it keeps to its allotted season. Forced chrysanthemums in spring and summer are not welcome. Here are my feelings on the subject, addressed, tactfully, I hope, to the flower, trusting that the message will be passed on to the appropriate quarters.

> Be dumb, chrysanthemum,
> And do not offer me your blooms until
> Your season; for reason
> That I need them with wood fires and shortened days,
> To comfort me when yet another summer's gone,
> And I bereft, with nothing left
> But chill and haze and flying leaves
> To feed my senses on.
>
> So keep your treasures till their time and do not show
> Your curly mops in shops
> In June, too soon.

The smell of chrysanthemums, which once belonged to autumn, together with the earthy smell of field mushrooms, is spoiled for me now, for both are an everyday commodity, obtainable all the year round. Once I could never bring myself to throw a dead chrysanthemum on to the compost heap. Always I saved them to burn on the first open fires of winter, so that their astringent perfume could be savoured to the last. But Osbert Sitwell has made me question the wisdom of this romantic gesture. 'These with a noxious smell — as, for instance, the chrysanthemum – should at all costs be avoided,' he says. 'Dank, damp chrysanthemums, whose petals give out no light, but instead seem to withdraw it from the air around them: chrysanthemums, which in their art-shades of mauve and terra-cotta and russet, smell of moths, camphor balls and drowned sailors, or white chrysanthemums that appear to be covered with hair rather than petals, and to resemble Aberdeen terriers and Sealyhams rather than a flower.'[1]

Beverley Nichols, with a little more restraint, describes the scent as one of the few masculine perfumes of nature. Addington Symonds likens it to honied heliotrope, and V. S. Fletcher agrees about the honey smell, but really we have no words for scents; we can only liken one scent to another, or contrast them. What dictionary contains a word for the delicious smell of tomato leaves rubbed between the fingers, or the pungent foreign-ness of a chrysanthemum? One man's heliotrope is another man's drowned sailor.

The chrysanthemum is a native of China, and has been cultivated in China and Japan for at least two thousand years. It became the personal emblem of the Mikado, and was represented on the Japanese flag and on their postage stamps. It is one of the most popular flowers in Japanese and Chinese art.

By the seventeenth century the first plants had found their way to Holland; and they reached England in 1764, when Phillip Miller grew them in the Botanic Garden in Chelsea. A purple variety was brought to France by Mons. Blanchard, a merchant of Marseilles, in 1789, and this reached England in 1795.

The founder of the Chrysanthemum Society was Robert James, regarded as the father of the chrysanthemum; and the first chrysanthemum show was held in Norwich in 1843. The name is derived from the Greek and means a gold flower, because the most familiar to the Greeks was gold.

To balance Osbert Sitwell's anti-chrysanthemumism, here is a passage from Maeterlinck. 'Autumn gives them all the mud-brown work of the rain in the woods, all the silvery fashionings of the mist in the plains, of the frost and snow in the gardens. . . . It allows them to deck themselves with the golden sequins, the bronze medals, the silver buckles, the copper spangles, the elfin plumes, the powdered amber, the burnt topazes, the neglected pearls, the smoked amethysts, the calcined garnets, all the dead but still dazzling jewellery which the north wind heaps up in the hollows of ravines and footpaths.'[2]

But Thomas Hardy, as usual, brings us down to earth — garden earth — with 'The Last Chrysanthemum'.

> Through the slow summer, when the sun
> > Called to each frond and whorl
> That all he could do for flowers was being done,
> > Why did it not uncurl?

Alas, today the chrysanthemum uncurls obediently at the command of the nurseryman, and the sun, for all his might, can go whistle.

The Nosegay Gathered

And so our nosegay is gathered and loosely tied, with regret for the lupins, the phlox, the sweet peas, and all the other common flowers for which we could find no place.

Geraniums, as untutored gardeners such as I still insist on calling the genus pelargonium, are tender, and driven to skulking under beds and on the tops of cupboards for the winter months, and therefore cannot be included among our sturdy cottagers. I am not really sorry, for geraniums are great quarrellers in mixed bunches.

A problem common to all writers, painters and gardeners is — what to leave out. Givers of parties, too, will understand my dilemma; for hospitality, as they well know, can be overdone. There comes a time, even in the most crowded cottage garden, when one must firmly shut the gate and say,

> The time is come. I can no more
> The vegetable world explore.[1]

*   *   *

> Farewell, dear flowers, sweetly your time ye spent,
> Fit, while ye lived, for smell or ornament,
>   And after death, for cures;
> I follow straight without complaint or grief,
> Since if my scent be good, I care not if
>   It be as short as yours.

GEORGE HERBERT.

Acknowledgements

The author would like to express her gratitude for permission to quote from the following works:

GEOFFREY BLES LTD. *Content with what I have* by C. Henry Warren;

JONATHAN CAPE LTD. and Mr F. R. Fletcher *Kilvert's Diary* ed. by William Plomer;

JONATHAN CAPE LTD. and the Executors of the Mary Webb Estate *Precious Bane, Gone to Earth, Poems and the Spring of Joy* by Mary Webb;

GERALD DUCKWORTH & CO. LTD. *Light and Twilight* by Edward Thomas;

FABER AND FABER LTD. *Country Hoard* by Alison Uttley;

JOHN GIFFORD LTD. Verse by J. E. Spingarn from *Garden Clematis* by Stanley Whitehead;

THE MANCHESTER GUARDIAN *Spears in the Soil* by Jason Hill;

THE HAMLYN PUBLISHING GROUP LIMITED 'Farm Holiday' from *Saturday to Monday* by Katharin McIntosh;

WILLIAM HEINEMANN LTD. and the Estate of the late Richard Church 'The Death of the Irises' from *Collected Poems* by Richard Church;

WILLIAM HEINEMANN LTD. Laurence Pollinger Ltd. and the Estate of the late Mrs Frieda Lawrence 'The Rose of England' from *The Complete Poems of D. H. Lawrence* and 'Flowery Tuscany' from *Phoenix* by D. H. Lawrence;

HODDER & STOUGHTON LTD. 'The Cowslip Fields' by George Ryland from *One Thousand Beautiful Things* ed. by Arthur Mee (London 1925);

THE HOGARTH PRESS *Cider with Rosie* by Laurie Lee;

HOUGHTON MIFFLIN COMPANY 'Lilacs' from *The Complete Poetical Works of Amy Lowell*;

GERALD HOWE LTD. *The Garden Book of Thomas Hanmer* ed. by Eleanour Sinclair Rohde;

205

MICHAEL JOSEPH LTD. Poem by Ralph Knevet from *Another World Than This* ed. by V. Sackville-West and Harold Nicolson;

MACDONALD AND CO. (Publishers) LTD. and the Estate of the late John Cowper Powys 'Whiteness' from *Collected Poems* by John Cowper Powys;

MACMILLAN, London and Basingstoke and the Trustees of the Hardy Estate 'The Lodging-House Fuchsias' and 'The Last Chrysanthemum' from *Collected Poems* by Thomas Hardy;

MACMILLAN, London and Basingstoke and David Higham Associates Ltd. *Penny Foolish* by Osbert Sitwell;

THE LITERARY TRUSTEES OF WALTER DE LA MARE and THE SOCIETY OF AUTHORS as their representative: 'The Snowdrop' and 'The Miracle' from *Collected Poems* by Walter de la Mare;

THE SOCIETY OF AUTHORS as the literary representative of the Estate of John Masefield: Verses from *The Collected Poems*, *The Everlasting Mercy* and *Lollington Downs* by John Masefield;

METHUEN AND CO. LTD. 'The Dormouse and The Doctor' from *When We Were Very Young* by A. A. Milne;

JOHN MURRAY (Publishers) LTD. *The Thread of Gold* by A. C. Benson;

OXFORD UNIVERSITY PRESS *Larkrise to Candleford* by Flora Thompson;

THE ROYAL SOCIETY FOR THE PROTECTION OF BIRDS, and THE SOCIETY of AUTHORS: *A Shepherd's Life* and *Book of a Naturalist* by W. H. Hudson;

THE ESTATE OF V. SACKVILLE-WEST and MICHAEL JOSEPH LTD. *The Garden* by V. Sackville-West;

SIDGWICK & JACKSON LTD. 'Persuasion' from *Collected Poems of John Drinkwater*;

GEORGE WEIDENFELD AND NICOLSON *For a Flower Album* by Colette.

Gratitude is also due to Mrs Mary Hillier for her help, and I would ask forgiveness from anyone whose rights I may have inadvertently overlooked, or whose sources I have failed to find.

Sources of Quotations

All mentions of Culpeper, Gerard or Parkinson in the text refer to:

Nicholas Culpeper *Complete Herbal* (Manchester 1826)
John Gerard *Herball* (3rd ed. London 1633)
John Parkinson *Paradisi in Sole Paradisus Terrestris* (London 1629)

POORMAN'S NOSEGAY

1. Andrew Tuer *Old London Street Cries* (London 1885)
2. Richard Weston *The Gardener's and Planter's Calendar* (London 1773)
3. Anne Manning *Deborah's Diary* (London c. 1908)
4. Sir Hugh Platt *The Jewell House of Art and Nature* (London 1594)
5. Levimus Leminius (1560) from *A History of Gardening in England* by Alicia Amhurst (London 1896)
6. Michael Drayton 'The Ballad of Dowsabell' from *The London Book of English Verse* (London 1953)
7. William Browne from *In Praise of Flowers* Ed. Neville Hilditch (London 1954)
8. Anon *Nature Display'd* Trans. Samuel Humphreys (London 1766)
9. Geoffrey Chaucer 'The Romaunt of the Rose' from *Gardens* by Sir William Beach Thomas (London 1952)
10. V. Sackville-West *Knole and the Sackvilles* (London 1933)
11. John Gay *The Beggar's Opera* (London 1921)
12. Henry Phillips *Flora Historica* (London 1824)
13. Henry Mayhew *Mayhew's London* Ed. Peter Quennell (London 1949)
14. Mrs. F. A. Bardswell *The Book of Town and Window Gardening* (London 1903)

THE COTTAGE PLOT

1. Holinshed *Chronicles* (London 1577)
2. Ralph Knevet 'The Vote' from *Another World Than This* Ed. V. Sackville-West and Harold Nicolson (London 1946)
3. Richard Barnfield 'The Affectionate Shepherd' from *Elizabethan Lyrics* Ed. Norman Ault (London 1925)
4. John Clare *Joys of the Garden* Ed. Sidney Shaylor (London)
5. William Cobbett *Rural Rides* (London 1853)
6. Thomas Bewick *Memoirs* Ed. Montague Weekley (London 1961)
7. Charles Marshall *Advice to Young Gardeners* (London 1808)
8. Anon *Cottage Gardening* (London 1882)
9. Dion Clayton Calthrop *The Charm of Gardens* (London 1910)
10. Maurice Maeterlinck *Old Fashioned Flowers* (London 1906)
11. A. C. Benson *The Thread of Gold* (London 1916)
12. W. H. Hudson *A Shepherd's Life* (London 1961)
13. A. E. Coppard 'Luxury' from *Selected Tales* (London 1949)
14. Katharin McIntosh 'Farm Holiday' from *Saturday to Monday* Ed. Frank Whittaker and W. T. Williams (London 1938)

POORMAN'S PLEASURE GARDEN

1. Thomas Tusser *His Good Points of Husbandry* Ed. Dorothy Hartley (London 1931)
2. J. Worlidge 'Systema Horticulturae' from *Gardener's Weekend Book* Ed. Eleanour Sinclair Rohde and Eric Parker (London)
3. Thomas Fairchild *The City Gardener* (London 1722)
4. William Hone *Hone's Every-Day Book* (London 1842)
5. Parson Woodforde *Diary of a Country Parson 1758–1802* Ed. Beresford (London 1949)
6. 'The Carthusian' 'The Poetry of Gardening' from *The Praise of Gardens* Ed. Albert Sieveking (London 1885)
7. Henry Mayhew *Mayhew's London* Ed. Peter Quennell (London 1949)
8. Dion Clayton Calthrop *The Charm of Gardens* (London 1910)

9. Leigh Hunt *Autobiography 1784–1859* (London 1860)
10. Thomas Moore *Life of Lord Byron with his Letters and Journals* (London 1844)
11. Anon *The Parlour Gardener* (London 1863)
12. Charles Dickens *Sketches by Boz* (London 1894)
13. Mrs. F. A. Bardswell *The Book of Town and Window Gardening* (London 1903)
14. Alexander Shand *Memories of Gardens* (London 1910)
15. Compton Mackenzie 'The Passionate Elopement' from the *Oxford Book of English Prose* Ed. Sir Arthur Quiller-Couch (London 1925)

SNOWDROP

1. Anon 'An Early Calendar of English Flowers' from *Flowers and Flower Lore* by Rev. Hilderic Friend (London 1884)
2. Jason Hill 'Spears in the Soil' *The Manchester Guardian*
3. William Morris *Hopes and Fears for Art* (London 1885)
4. Anon 'The Day Book of Melisande' from *The Garden of Delight* Ed. John Richardson (London 1912)
5. Mary Webb 'The Snowdrop' from *Poems and the Spring of Joy* (London 1929)
6. Walter de la Mare 'The Snowdrop' from *Collected Poems* (London 1961)

CROCUS

1. Richard Hakluyt *Voyages* (London)
2. D. H. Lawrence *Flowery Tuscany* (London)
3. E.V.B. (Hon. Mrs. Evelyn Boyle) *Days and Hours in a Garden* (London 1890)
4. Harriet Martineau *Autobiography* (London 1877)

DAFFODIL

1. Dion Clayton Calthrop *The Charm of Gardens* (London 1910)
2. Canon Vaughan *The Music of Wild Flowers* (London 1920)

3. Dorothy Wordsworth *Dove Cottage, The Wordsworths at Grasmere 1799–1803* Ed. Kingsley Hart (London 1966)
4. Austin Dobson from *The Romance of Garden Flowers* by Hilda M. Coley (London 1948)
5. Colette *For a Flower Album* Trans. Roger Senhouse (London 1959)
6. Addison 'The Tatler, no. 218' from *The Praise of Gardens* Ed. Albert Sieveking (London 1885)
7. Oscar Wilde from *In a City Garden* by J. R. Aitken (London 1913)

TULIP

1. Dion Clayton Calthrop *The Charm of Gardens* (London 1910)
2. Colette *For a Flower Album* Trans. Roger Senhouse (London 1959)
3. Anon *Nature Display'd* Trans. Samuel Humphreys (London 1766)
4. Thomas Hanmer *Garden Book* Intro. Eleanour Sinclair Rohde (London 1933)
5. Thomas Miller *The Language of Flowers or The Pilgrimage of Love* (London 1862)
6. Alphonse Karr *A Tour Round My Garden* Trans. Rev. J. G. Wood (London 1859)
7. James Shirley *The Gentleman of Venice* (London 1655)
8. Alexander Dumas the elder *The Black Tulip* (London 1904)
9. John Parkinson *Paradisi in Sole Paradisus Terrestris* (London 1629)

PRIMROSE

1. Shakespeare *The Winter's Tale* Act IV Sc. III (London 1915)
2. Mary Webb *Poems and the Spring of Joy* (London c. 1928)
3. Reginald Farrer from *The Garden Book* Ed. Anne Lamplugh (London 1937)
4. Mrs. F. A. Bardswell *The Book of Town and Window Gardening* (London 1903)
5. Elizabeth (Countess Russell) *Elizabeth and her German Garden* (London 1899)
6. Izaak Walton *The Compleat Angler* (London 1949)

COWSLIP

1. Izaak Walton *The Compleat Angler* (London 1949)
2. William Turner *A New Herball* (London 1551)
3. Henry Lyte *A Nieue Herball* (London 1619)
4. Laurie Lee *Cider With Rosie* (London 1950)
5. Mrs. Plues *Rambles in Search of Wild Flowers* (London 1863)
6. Thomas Miller *Common Wayside Flowers* (London 1863)
7. Mary Webb *Precious Bane* (London 1928)
8. Edward Thomas *Light and Twilight* (London)
9. George Ryland 'The Cowslip Fields' from *One Thousand Beautiful Things* Ed. Arthur Mee (London 1925)
10. Richard Church *Calling For a Spade* (London 1939)

AURICULA

1. John Loudon *Encyclopaedia of Gardening* (London 1822)
2. Thomas Hanmer *Garden Book* Intro. Eleanour Sinclair Rohde (London 1933)

WALLFLOWER

1. Canon Vaughan *The Music of Wild Flowers* (London 1920)
2. John Clare *Shepherd's Calendar* Ed. Eric Robinson and Geoffrey Summerfield (London 1964)
3. Gervase Markham from *The Romance of Garden Flowers* by Hilda M. Coley (London 1948)
4. Robert Herrick 'How the Wall-flower Came First' from *Hesperides and Noble Numbers* (London 1923)
5. V. Sackville-West *The Garden* (London)

DAISY

1. Giles Fletcher the younger 'Easter Morn' from *Elizabethan Lyrics* Ed. Norman Ault (London 1925)

2. Chaucer 'Prologue to the Legende of Good Women' from *Romance of Nature* by Louisa Anne Twamley (London 1836)
3. Andrew Young *A Prospect of Flowers* (London 1946)
4. W. H. Hudson *The Book of a Naturalist* (London)
5. E. Cobham Brewer *Dictionary of Phrase and Fable* (London 1901)
6. T. F. Thistleton Dyer *The Folklore of Plants* (London 1889)
7. William Wordsworth 'To the Same Flower' from *Poetical Works* (London)

ANEMONE

1. D. H. Lawrence *Flowery Tuscany* (London)
2. 'Sir' John Hill *Eden: or, a Compleat Body of Gardening* (London 1757)
3. Edward FitzGerald *Letters* Ed. Cohen (London 1960)
4. Henry Phillips *Flora Historica* (London 1824)
5. William Turner *A New Herball* (London 1551)

VIOLET

1. Alphonse Karr *A Tour Round My Garden* Trans. Rev. J. G. Wood (London 1859)
2. Dorothy Hewlett *Adonais* (London 1927)
3. Henry Lyte *A Nieue Herball* (London 1578)
4. Tyler Whittle *Common or Garden* (London 1969)
5. Charles Lamb 'Mackery End' from *Essays of Elia. Vol.* 1 (London 1914)
6. W. Wilmot Dixon *Dainty Ladies of Society* (London 1903)
7. William Cobbett *Rural Rides* (London 1853)
8. Thomas Miller *Common Wayside Flowers* (London 1880)
9. John Masefield *Collected Poems* (London 1929)
10. Robert Herrick 'Upon Prew, His Maid' from *Hesperides and Noble Numbers* (London 1923)

PANSY

1. Leigh Hunt 'Descent of Liberty' from *Flora Symbolica* by John Ingram (London)
2. Bullein's *Bulwarke of Defence* (London 1562)
3. Henry Phillips *Flora Historica* (London 1824)
4. 'Handasyde' *The Four Gardens* (London 1924)
5. Elizabeth (Countess Russell) *Fräulein Schmidt and Mr. Anstruther* (London 1899)

FORGET-ME-NOT

1. John Gerard *Herball* (3rd ed. London 1633)

LILY OF THE VALLEY

1. Edward Hume *Familiar Wild Flowers* (London)
2. Henry Phillips *Flora Historica* (London 1824)
3. James Hurdis 'The Lily of the Valley' from *In the Garden of Delight* Ed. John Richardson (London 1912)

CROWN IMPERIAL

1. John Parkinson *Paradisi in Sole Paradisus Terrestris* (London 1629)
2. Alfred Austin *In Veronica's Garden* (London 1897)
3. Mrs. C. W. Earle *Pot-Pourri From a Surrey Garden* (London 1897)
4. E.V.B. (Hon. Mrs. Evelyn Boyle) *A Garden of Pleasure* (London 1895)
5. Fr. René Rapin *Of Gardens* Trans. John Evelyn (London 1673)

FRITILLARY

1. V. Sackville-West *The Garden* (London 1946)
2. John Parkinson *Paradisi in Sole Paradisus Terrestris* (London 1629)
3. Geoffrey Grigson *Wild Flowers in Britain* (London 1942)

IRIS

1. Anne Pratt *Haunts of the Wild Flowers* (London)
2. E.V.B. (Hon. Mrs. Evelyn Boyle) *A Garden of Pleasure* (London 1895)
3. D. H. Lawrence *Flowery Tuscany* (London)
4. Richard Church 'The Death of the Irises' from *News From the Mountain* (London 1932)

COLUMBINE

1. John Gerard *Herball* (3rd ed. London 1633)
2. W. H. Hudson *The Book of a Naturalist* (London)
3. John Clare 'Shepherd's Calendar' from *My Kalendar of Country Delights* by Helen Milman (London 1903)
4. John Parkinson *Paradisi in Sole Paradisus Terrestris* (London 1629)

HONEYSUCKLE

1. Anon from *Flowers of the Woods and Hedges* by Anne Pratt (London)
2. John Parkinson *Paradisi in Sole Paradisus Terrestris* (London 1629)
3. Helen Milman *My Kalendar of Country Delights* (London 1903)
4. Walter Savage Landor from *Joys of the Garden* Ed. Sidney J. Shaylor (London)

PEONY

1. William Coles *Adam and Eve, or Nature's Paradise* (London 1657)
2. Nicholas Culpeper *Complete Herbal* (Manchester 1826)

LILAC

1. Mary Webb *Gone to Earth* (London 1928)
2. Elizabeth (Countess Russell) *Elizabeth and her German Garden* (London 1899)
3. William Cowper from *Flora Symbolica* by John Ingram (London)
4. Amy Lowell 'Lilacs' from *The Complete Poetical Works* (Boston U.S.A.)
5. Lizette Woodworth Reese 'Lydia is Gone This Many a Year' from *Come Hither* Ed. Walter de la Mare (London 1923)

RANUNCULUS

1. Anon *Nature Display'd* Trans. Samuel Humphreys (London 1766)
2. Thomas Hogg *A Concise and Practical Treatise on the Growth and Culture of the Carnation, Pink, Auricula, etc.* (Middlesex 1824)
3. Una Sylberrad and Sophie Lyall *Dutch Bulbs and Gardens* (London 1909)

CLEMATIS

1. John Parkinson *Paradisi in Sole Paradisus Terrestris* (London 1629)
2. Mary Pirie *A Popular Book on Flowers, Grasses and Shrubs* (London 1865)
3. Thomas Hanmer *Garden Book* Intro. Eleanour Sinclair Rohde (London 1933)
4. John Clare from *Haunts of the Wild Flowers* by Anne Pratt (London 1890)
5. Emilie and Georges Romieu *The Life of George Eliot* (London 1932)

CARNATION

1. William Cobbett *The American Gardener* (London 1824)

2. Francis Brett Young 'Prothalamium' from *Georgian Poetry* 1918–1919
3. Nicholas Culpeper *Complete Herbal* (Manchester 1826)
4. Walter de la Mare 'About and Roundabout' from *Come Hither* (London 1923)
5. Sir Herbert Maxwell *Scottish Gardens* (London 1908)
6. Marion Henderson *My Garden's Bedside Book* Ed. Theo Stephens (Guildford)
7. Fr. René Rapin *Of Gardens* Trans. John Evelyn (London 1673)

PINK

1. Henry Lyte *A Nieue Herball* (London 1578)
2. Thomas Ibbett 'On the Origin of the Pink' from *The Floricultural Cabinet* (London 1841)
3. John Clare *Shepherd's Calendar* (London 1964)

SWEET WILLIAM

1. John Parkinson *Paradisi in Sole Paradisus Terrestris* (London 1629)
2. John Gerard *Herball* (3rd ed. London 1633)
3. Rev. Henry Bright *A Year in a Lancashire Garden* (London 1891)

MARIGOLD

1. Bartolomaeus Anglicus *The Grete Herball* (London 1526)
2. Joseph Hall, Bishop of Exeter and Norwich 'Occasional Meditations' from *The Praise of Gardens* Ed. Albert Sieveking (London 1885)
3. Charles Lamb 'Christ's Hospital Thirty Years Ago' from *Essays of Elia, Vol.* 1 Ed. William Macdonald (London 1914)
4. W. H. Hudson *A Shepherd's Life* (London 1961)
5. Charles I 'Flowers Drawn From Nature' from *Spaendonck* Ed. Wilfrid Blunt (London 1957)

SOURCES OF QUOTATIONS

HOLLYHOCK

1. Henry Phillips *Flora Historica* (London 1824)
2. Anon from *Flora Symbolica* by John Ingram (London)
3. Maurice Maeterlinck *Old Fashioned Flowers* (London 1906)
4. Walter de la Mare 'The Miracle' from *Collected Poems* (London 1961)

SNAPDRAGON

1. Walter de la Mare *Memoirs of a Midget* (London 1932)
2. Louisa Anne Twamley *Our Wild Flowers* (London 1839)
3. Henry Phillips *Flora Historica* (London 1824)
4. Walter de la Mare 'About and Roundabout' from *Come Hither* (London 1923)

LARKSPUR AND DELPHINIUM

1. John Gerard *Herball* (3rd ed. London 1633)
2. John Parkinson *Paradisi in Sole Paradisus Terrestris* (London 1629)
3. John Clare *Shepherd's Calendar* (London 1964)

FOXGLOVE

1. William Turner from *Flora Historica* by Henry Phillips (London 1824)
2. John Gerard *Herball* (3rd ed. London 1633)
3. Anon *Wild Flowers of the Year* (London)
4. Anne Pratt *Flowers of the Woods and Hedges* (London 1846)
5. Alison Uttley *Country Hoard* (London 1953)
6. Mary Webb *Precious Bane* (London 1928)
7. Beverley Nichols *Down the Garden Path* (London 1938)
8. Shakespeare *Romeo and Juliet* Act II Sc. III (London 1915)

LOVE-IN-A-MIST

1. Maurice Maeterlinck 'The Intelligence of Flowers' from *Life and Flowers* (London 1907)

CORNFLOWER

1. Nicholas Culpeper *Complete Herbal* (Manchester 1826)
2. Andrew Young *Retrospect of Flowers* (London 1950)
3. Henry Warren *Content With What I Have* (London 1968)

POPPY

1. Alphonse Karr *A Tour Round My Garden* Trans. Rev. J. G. Wood (London 1859)
2. John McCrae from *Flowers in History* by Peter Coats (London 1970)
3. William Cobbett *Rural Rides* (London 1853)
4. Anon 'An Early Calendar of English Flowers' from *Flowers and Flower Lore* by Rev. Hilderic Friend (London 1884)
5. John Parkinson *Paradisi in Sole Paradisus Terrestris* (London 1629)
6. Lady Wilkinson *Weeds and Wild Flowers: Their Uses, Legends and Literature* (London 1858)
7. John Ruskin *The Garden of Proserpine* (London)
8. Alexander Neckham, Abbot of Cirencester 'Of the Nature of Things' from *The Praise of Gardens* Ed. Albert Sieveking (London 1885)
9. Leonard Meager *The New Art of Gardening* (London 1699)

STOCK

1. Mrs. Loudon from *Flowers in History* by Alice Coats (London 1956)

DAME'S VIOLET

1. W. Davenport Adams *The Book of English Epigrams* (London)
2. Wilfrid Blunt *The Art of Botanical Illustration* (London 1955)
3. H. M. Batson *A Book of the Country and the Garden* (London 1903)

MONKSHOOD

1. Richard Bradley *Planting and Gardening* (London 1724)
2. Henry Phillips *Flora Historica* (London 1824)
3. Andrew Young *A Retrospect of Flowers* (London 1946)
4. Robert Southey 'The Doctor' from *The Praise of Gardens* Ed. Albert Sieveking (London 1885)
5. John Keats 'Ode on Melancholy' from *Oxford Book of English Verse* Ed. Arthur Quiller-Couch (London 1916)
6. Shakespeare *King Henry IV* Part II (London 1915)

MIGNONETTE

1. V. Sackville-West *The Garden* (London 1946)
2. Alison Uttley *Country Hoard* (London 1943)

LILY

1. Francis Quarles *In Praise of Flowers* Ed. Neville Hilditch (London 1954)
2. Alfred Tennyson 'Balin and Balan' from *The Works of Alfred Lord Tennyson* (London 1894)
3. John Masefield *Collected Poems* (London 1929)
4. Rev. Henry Bright *A Year in a Lancashire Garden* (London 1891)
5. Maurice Maeterlinck *Old Fashioned Flowers* (London 1906)
6. Mary Webb 'Roots' from *Poems and the Spring of Joy* (London c.1928)
7. Dion Clayton Calthrop *The Charm of Gardens* (London 1910)
8. Spenser 'Fairie Queene Bk. II' from *Elizabethan Lyrics* Ed. Norman Ault (London 1925)

ROSE

1. Alfred Tennyson 'Becket Act II' *The Works of Alfred Lord Tennyson* (London 1894)
2. D. H. Lawrence 'The Rose of England' from *Pansies* (London 1932)
3. Barry Cornwall from *My Kalendar of Country Delights* by Helen Milman (London 1903)
4. Dean Hole *A Book About Roses* (London 1896)
5. John Wilkes 'Letter to his Daughter' from *The Praise of Gardens* Ed. Albert Sieveking (London 1885)
6. Alfred Austin *The Garden That I Love* (London 1906)
7. George Eliot from *The Garden Book* Ed. Anne Lamplugh (London 1937)

THE RED ROSE

1. John Masefield 'Lollington Downs' from *Georgian Poetry* 1916–1917

THE WHITE ROSE

1. Shakespeare *Henry VI Part I* Act II Sc. IV (London 1915)
2. Anon *Flower Lore* (Belfast)
3. E.V.B. (Hon. Mrs. Evelyn Boyle) *A Garden of Pleasure* (London 1895)
4. Christina Rossetti *Songs for Strangers and Pilgrims* (London 1884)
5. John Gerard *Herball* (3rd ed. London 1633)
6. J. C. Powys 'Whiteness' from *Poems* (London 1964)

THE BRIAR ROSE

1. Shakespeare *Romeo and Juliet* Act V Sc. I (London 1915)
2. William Beckford 'Letter of May 10th 1787' from *The Praise of Gardens* Ed. Albert Sieveking (London 1895)

3. E.V.B. (Hon. Mrs. Evelyn Boyle) *A Garden of Pleasure* (London 1895)

ROSEMARY

1. John Evelyn 'Fumifugium; or the Inconveniences of the aer and smoak of London dissipated' from *The Book of the Garden* by Arthur Stanley (London 1932)
2. Sir Thomas More from *The Household of Sir Thomas More* by Anne Manning (London)
3. Robert Herrick 'The Rosemarie Branch' from *Hesperides and Noble Numbers* (London 1923)
4. Rev. Hilderic Friend *Flowers and Flower Lore* (London 1884)
5. Mary Webb *Precious Bane* (London 1928)
6. Bancke's *Herbal* (London 1525)

LAVENDER

1. William Turner *Herball* (London 1568)
2. John Parkinson *Paradisi in Sole Paradisus Terrestris* (London 1629)
3. Izaak Walton *The Compleat Angler* (London 1949)
4. E. T. Cook *Gardens of England* (London 1923)
5. William Hunnis (?) from *Elizabethan Lyrics* Ed. Norman Ault (London 1925)
6. Michael Drayton 'Pastorals' from *Eclogue IX* (London)

PERIWINKLE

1. Rev. Hilderic Friend *Flowers and Flower Lore* (London 1884)
2. Mary Webb *Poems and the Spring of Joy* (London *c.* 1928)
3. Rev. Henry Ellacombe *In a Gloucestershire Garden* (London 1896)

FUCHSIA

1. Rev. Henry Ellacombe *In a Gloucestershire Garden* (London 1896)
2. Mary Webb *Gone to Earth* (London 1928)

SUNFLOWER

1. E.V.B. (Hon. Mrs. Evelyn Boyle) *Days and Hours in a Garden* (London 1890)

CHRYSANTHEMUM

1. Osbert Sitwell *Penny Foolish* (London 1935)
2. Maurice Maeterlinck *Old Fashioned Flowers* (London 1906)

THE NOSEGAY GATHERED

1. Mrs. Delaney 'A Farewell to her paper Flora, on the approach of blindness, 1782' from *Aspasia* by C. E. Vulliamy (London 1935)